The edition of *The Complete Works of Frances Ridley Havergal* has five parts:

Volume I   *Behold Your King: The Complete Poetical Works of Frances Ridley Havergal*

Volume II   *Whose I Am and Whom I Serve: Prose Works of Frances Ridley Havergal*

Volume III *Loving Messages for the Little Ones: Works for Children by Frances Ridley Havergal*

Volume IV   *Love for Love: Frances Ridley Havergal: Memorials, Letters and Biographical Works*

Volume V   *Songs of Truth and Love: Music by Frances Ridley Havergal and William Henry Havergal*

David L. Chalkley, Editor   Dr. Glen T. Wegge, Music Editor

Frances Ridley Havergal's formal education ended when she was 17, with one term at a young women's school in Düsseldorf, Germany, yet she was a true scholar all her life. Fluent in German and French and nearly so in Italian, she read and loved the Reformers in Latin, German, and French. Knowledge was never an end in itself, only a means to know better her Lord and Saviour and to help to bring others to know Him. The Bible was her only Book, and she studied the Hebrew and Greek texts of Scripture, memorized nearly all the New Testament and large portions of the Old Testament, and loved the Author with all her being.

Frances was brought to a saving knowledge of Christ when she was 14, and the rest of her life was consecrated to her Saviour, the Lord Jesus. Keenly aware of her own sinfulness and inability, her sole desire was to please and glorify Him alone. Very finely gifted, she was truly diligent with her gifts: her poetry is among the finest in the English language, after George Herbert; her prose works are deeply beneficial; a musician to the core, she left behind important compositions. Like her works, her life richly touched the ones near her and countless many who met or heard her. The Lord Jesus Christ was her alone, only beauty, and she glowed Him and His truth. Never wanting attention to herself, Frances' desire of her heart was for herself and for others to know her King, the Lord Jesus Christ. Her works are a gold-mine of help and enrichment. There is life in these pages: her works truly glorify the Lord, truly benefit His people, and powerfully reach those who do not yet know Him.

The Music of Frances Ridley Havergal by Glen T. Wegge, Ph.D.

This Companion Volume to the Havergal edition is a valuable presentation of F.R.H.'s scores, most or nearly all of F.R.H.'s scores very little if any at all seen, or even known of, for nearly a century. What a valuable body of music has been unknown for so long and is now made available to many. Dr. Wegge completed his Ph.D. in Music Theory at Indiana University at Bloomington, and his diligence and thoroughness in this volume are obvious. First an analysis of F.R.H.'s compositions is given, an essay that both addresses the most advanced musicians and also reaches those who are untrained in music; then all the extant scores that have been found are newly typeset, with complete texts for each score and extensive indices at the end of the book. This volume presents F.R.H.'s music in newly typeset scores diligently prepared by Dr. Wegge, and Volume V of the Havergal edition presents the scores in facsimile, the original 19th century scores. (The essay—a dissertation—analysing her scores is given the same both in this Companion Volume and in Volume V of the Havergal edition.)

Dr. Wegge is also preparing all of these scores for publication in performance folio editions.

The Havergal Trust   P.O.Box 649   Kirksville, Missouri 63501

William Henry Havergal (1793–1870) was the foremost church musician and composer of sacred music in England in his generation. A finely gifted performer and music leader, he composed and published important music, and was a leading reformer of church music practice. He was offered a professorship in music at Oxford University, but he declined that for his first calling, to be a minister and pastor. Though rarely gifted to write music, he preferred to prepare a sermon than to compose a score. Music was a very important part of his ministry, and always a pleasure and rest to him, but he concentrated on music only when his physical health prevented him from his pastoral work. His Sermons, printed in four volumes, are gold. He was the most important musical mentor to his daughter, Frances Ridley Havergal.

This is a photograph taken by (the prestigious portrait photographers) Elliott and Fry in London on February 1, 1879, one of eight taken of F.R.H. that day by them. In a letter dated February 7, 1879, F.R.H. wrote this: "I have been photographed! Mr. Elliott himself came for me, Saturday, and they tried eight times, and hope one will do! Elliott and Fry both superintended in person; such a fuss! And I forgot to put on tidy frill and cuffs!" (in Division VI of Letters by the Late Frances Ridley Havergal, *page 312; page 232 of Volume IV of the Havergal edition) This would have been Saturday, February 1, 1879, a month and a half after her 42nd birthday and four months before her unexpected early death on June 3.*

No. 163.

the last music by W.H.H.

Havergal. 777, 777, 777.

(See Preface, p. xxi.)

[124]

W. H. H., April 16, 1870.

Migh - ty Fa - ther! Bless - ed Son! Ho - ly Spi - rit! Three in One! E - ver -

- more Thy will be done! Threefold is Thy glo-rious might, Three-fold is Thy

name of light, Ho - ly! Aw - ful! In - fi - nite! Three-fold let our prai-ses be,

Great mys - te - rious One, to Thee! Un - di - vi - ded Tri - ni - ty! A - men.

This is Number 163 in Havergal's Psalmody and Century of Chants, and the score for hymn number 4 in the companion Songs of Grace and Glory. This manuscript was the last music score composed by William Henry Havergal, composed on his last conscious day, Saturday, April 16, 1870. The text by Dr. John S. B. Monsell is symbolic of the Trinity, having three lines in each verse, three verses in each section, and three sections for one hymn. This score was named "Havergal," and his daughter Frances Ridley Havergal wrote, "The tune with its serene melody and rich harmony is itself an epitome of his musical work" (Specimen Glasses for the King's Minstrels by Frances Ridley Havergal, London: Home Words Publishing Office, 1881), original book pages 109–110, page 765 of Volume II of the Havergal edition. See page xii of this book.

Havergal's Psalmody and Century of Chants.

FROM

"Old Church Psalmody."
"Hundred Tunes" & Unpublished Manuscripts.

OF THE LATE

Rev. W. H. Havergal, M.A.

Honorary Canon of Worcester

with Prefaces, Indices and Portrait.

Edited by his daughter, Frances Ridley Havegal.

The Original 1871 Edition Published by Robert Cocks & Co., London

Taken from the New Edition of
The Complete Works of Frances Ridley Havergal

" Knowing her intense desire that Christ should be magnified, whether
by her life or in her death, may it be to His glory
that in these pages she, being dead,
'Yet speaketh!'"

HAVERGAL'S PSALMODY AND CENTURY OF CHANTS.
by William Henry Havergal, edited by Frances Ridley Havergal
Copyright © 2017 by the Havergal Trust.

ISBN 978-1-937236-55-7   Library of Congress Control Number: 2016919856

Printed in the United States of America   *This book is printed on acid-free paper.*

Cover Design by Glen T. Wegge.

Havergal, Frances Ridley
Songs of Truth and Love: prose, poetry, and music taken from the edition of the
complete works of Frances Ridley Havergal / Frances Ridley Havergal. 1. Havergal,
Frances Ridley, 1836–1879. 2. Christian Life. 3. Christian Poetry, English. 4.
Music. I. Title

This is taken from *The Complete Works of Frances Ridley Havergal.*
David L. Chalkley, General Editor.   Dr. Glen T. Wegge, Music Editor.

The purpose of this work is ministry, and any money received by the Havergal Trust from sales of these books is to be applied to con-
tinue the work of the Trust, all revenues being applied to cover true costs of production and distribution and then to publish and distrib-
ute more books more widely, with very affordable prices, with no financial profit to any involved beyond fair market compensation for
time and labor. The purpose of the Trust is to preserve far into the future (if our Lord does not return sooner) works by and about F.R.H.,
to make available to many these works, and to publish works by other authors similar to Havergal.

While most of the Havergal edition is made of public domain works published before 1923, throughout the edition are numerous
items of new work in 2003–2011.

Frances Ridley Havergal used language clearly, specifically, powerfully, precisely, and beautifully, and no alteration of any of her works
should be done. At the beginning of the 21st century her words are as simple and fresh as they were when she was here, and they should
be left precisely as she wrote them without any change.

Many valuable, important works have been gutted with a pretence of improving or clarifying the language, when the language of
Bonar, Spurgeon, Chambers, and others should be left alone in its original clarity, beauty, and power. F.R.H.'s sentences—and very
words—have a special power, clarity, beauty, sweetness, and precision which cannot be improved nor even matched—only harmed and
distorted—by any changes. Similarly, C. H. Spurgeon, J. C. Ryle, John Owen, John Flavel, Thomas Watson, George Whitefield, Jonathan Edwards, Robert Murray M'Cheyne, and many other similar authors should be left alone in their precise words they originally
wrote: any "improvement" of their precise words improves nothing, harms and distorts what they really said, and very often if not always
guts what they meant and invites things they never meant. This is far worse than "improving" paintings by Rembrandt, Vermeer, Monet
(which would be derided by anyone serious about art), or "improving" scores by Bach, Beethoven, or Rachmaninoff (any true musician
cleaves to the original scores with absolute fidelity to the tiniest notated details), and serious people would not accept such against Shake-
speare, Nathaniel Hawthorne, Goethe, nor such secular authors. It is a remarkable distortion for an editor to impose "trust me, I know
better" rather than the original author.

The photographs and illustrations should also be left just as they are, not "updated," "enhanced," nor changed in any way. ("Improving" Frances does not improve her.)

Many pieces such as "One Hour with Jesus," any of the poems, or other parts of this edition would be very beneficial to print in bul-
letins, periodicals, and other formats.

The Havergal Trust   P.O.Box 649   Kirksville, Missouri 63501

In all that she did, and in all that she wrote, Frances Ridley Havergal's one overriding desire was—as Colossians 1:18 says—"that in all things he [*her Lord*] might have the pre-eminence." She saw herself as an instrument in her Saviour's hand, writing for His sake, His glory alone. Indeed the words of Psalm 45:1 were true of her: "My heart is inditing a good matter: I speak of the things which I have made touching the King: my tongue is the pen of a ready writer."

The truth of Christ, which she so loved, and which He used her to present to others, is what is relevant and important, not Frances herself. Understanding the truth of this, you don't first of all think "what a wonderful, fine lady she was" but "what a Saviour ! she had." Jesus Christ alone was changing her from what she was, to become daily more like Himself. Frances would not want anyone to look solely or primarily at her, but she would want all to see her Lord and Saviour. He was her only beauty, righteousness, wisdom, her all. So as you embark on reading, may you too see the Lord Jesus Christ. To see her King is what she would have wanted, the true conclusion of her works and life, and of any genuine disciple's works and life. The Lamb is all the glory in Emmanuel's land, the kingdom of God.

A NOTE TO THE READER

Serious effort has been made to publish this edition of *The Complete Works of Frances Ridley Havergal* very closely to the original texts of F.R.H. When clear mistakes had been made in the original books, they were corrected without comment, and other, exceptional changes were made only when there was very good reason. Details of spelling and punctuation were preserved as they were found in the original works.

There were many inconsistencies in the original texts. For example, among different books, or even within the same book on occasion, "labour" and "endeavour" might also be spelled "labor" and "endeavor." Even among the original 19th century Havergal books published by James Nisbet & Co. (F.R.H.'s primary publisher), there is much inconsistency in the way quotation marks were done, consistent within the same book but different from one Nisbet book to another. The British way is to place quotations within single quotation marks, and to place quotations in quotations within double quotation marks: 'Jesus says, and says to you, "Come, oh come, to Me."' The American way is the reverse: "Jesus says, and says to you, 'Come, oh come, to Me.'" As this edition was typeset in 2004, the British way of quotation marks was used for the first item, the definitive, remarkably fine Nisbet edition of *The Poetical Works of Frances Ridley Havergal*, because this original volume used the British style of quotation marks. As we proceeded beyond Nisbet's *Poetical Works*, we saw that various original books alternated between the British and American styles, both among different books by the same publisher Nisbet, and also among other contemporary publishers of F.R.H. in the United Kingdom (Home Words Publishing Co. in London, Marcus Ward in Belfast, and others). Even a manuscript in Frances' own handwriting used the American way of quotation marks. Because there was a need for consistency (not an appearance of randomness or chaos), and because comparatively few are likely to see the pages of the original books, all the quotation marks in this edition are given in the American way, except for Nisbet's *Poetical Works*. Besides quotation marks, there were several other details that we would have done differently ourselves now in the 21st century, which we left the same as we found them in the original books.

If, in reading through these volumes, there is an *appearance* of randomness in the way the various works appear printed on the pages, we would ask that the reader please bear in mind that this edition was typeset using the *original* works: numerous volumes of poetry, prose (including biographies, sermons by Frances' father and others, etc.), and music by a number of different authors and publishers. As much as was practicable, considerable effort was made to make these works in this new edition "mirror" the original works—title pages, contents pages, etc.—even though we knew it is unlikely that the vast majority of readers will ever actually *see* these original works.

The desire and earnest effort was that this edition be an "urtext" edition, cleaving very closely to the original text. Exceptions were made when there was good reason, but these were rare. Perhaps the careful reader will also notice that most of the punctuation marks within the text of the Havergal edition have spacing inserted between them and adjacent letters and/or additional punctuation marks, reflecting typesetting practices of the 19th century. Significant effort was expended to accomplish this, the reason being, again, to cleave as closely as possible to the original text, as well as to give the finished version as much of an authentic look as practicable.

The important matter is, that we sought not to "improve" Frances (and her father, her sisters, and the others in this edition) but to present her as she originally wrote.

David Chalkley, Thomas Sadowski, Dr. Glen Wegge

For more than twelve years, Dr. Glen T. Wegge has been involved in the work to complete the Havergal edition. Without payment of money, with remarkable diligence, patience, persistence, and hard work, he has labored to prepare for publication all of the music in the Havergal edition, and also to complete and publish his own book, *The Music of Frances Ridley Havergal*, a Companion Volume to this edition of *The Complete Works of Frances Ridley Havergal*. He has also done so much to bring to completion (in countless hours of work) all of the other books in the Havergal edition. The patience and support of his wife, Denise, are also appreciated. So much thought, diligence, hard work, countless hours, a servant's heart, a labor of love. My estimate or guess is that Glen has worked approximately 1,500 hours on the Havergal edition, without pay. His work is remarkable both in quantity and in quality, first-rate, sterling work. How many times ? (the Lord knows how many times) has he gone back again and again to fix a text or an illustration until it was just right. Most of the details of his work were known only to Glen and me, much now forgotten, but God sees and knows every trace. How compassionately and richly He has blessed us in all of this.

For much or most of the past 100 years, few if any have realized the value of Frances' music, and Glen (who completed his Ph.D. in music theory at Indiana University at Bloomington and is so finely gifted and prepared to do this work) is the first one to analyze and present her music in such a scholarly way. He began his work on this in very difficult circumstances, and his diligence, persistence, and servant's heart are a true example for believers. Glen is worthy of strong gratitude from all those who will be encouraged and enriched by F.R.H.'s poetry, prose, and music.

The Lord reward him as I cannot, as no man can reward.

This is all the Lord's doing. Thanks be to God for His indescribable gift to us in Christ.

David Chalkley

The Complete Works of Frances Ridley Havergal is dedicated to the glory of the Lord Jesus Christ, laying this at His feet and asking Him to bless to others what He has provided,

"for Jesus' sake only"

and is gratefully inscribed to two people:

Miss Janet Grierson,
Mr. Stanley Ward.

Miss Grierson's Biography and her other work on F.R.H. are the most important work on Frances since Maria V. G. Havergal, and she has been invaluably helpful in the preparation of this edition.

Mr. Stanley Ward has been deeply interested in Frances since the 1960's, and his kindness, insights, and help have been truly and profoundly important to this edition.

Thanks be to God for His indescribable gift to us in Christ.

CONTENTS

Havergal's Psalmody and Century of Chants (the Fourth Edition published by James Nisbet & Co. in 1877, with a few items from the earlier 1871 edition published by Robert Cocks & Co.)

JUST PUBLISHED, PRICE TWO SHILLINGS,

Appendix

TO THE SIXTH EDITION OF THE

REVEREND W. H. HAVERGAL'S

Old Church Psalmody.

THIS small Volume, though nominally connected with one, the most valuable, of our Metrical Tune-Books, is really an "APPENDIX" to every Book of that class in use in English and American Churches and Chapels.

Mr Havergal's "OLD CHURCH PSALMODY," in its latest Edition, contained tunes for 27 different Metres, and few of the Tune-Books in general use contain more than that number: but the present "APPENDIX" contains Tunes for 49 Metres, to suit the translated German and other Hymns now so popular. These Tunes have all been contributed by "living Authors," and many of them have been "specially Composed" by the Rev. Sir F. A. GORE OUSELEY, Bart.; the Rev. W. H. HAVERGAL, and other well-known Church-musical writers: and will be found as worthy the notice of the most refined Choir for their scientific construction, as they are well adapted for Congregational use by their melodic simplicity.

LONDON:

ENOCH AND SONS, 19 HOLLES ST. CAVENDISH SQ. W.

The two separate volumes, Old Church Psalmody (1847) and A Hundred Psalm and Hymn Tunes, (1859) were published by W.H.H. while he lived. The date of this Appendix is not known. After he died, F.R.H. edited and published the definitive Havergal's Psalmody and Century of Chants (1871), adding a number of unpublished manuscript scores by her father and a number of scores composed by F.R.H.

This is Number 163 in *Havergal's Psalmody and Century of Chants*, and the score for hymn number 4 in the companion *Songs of Grace and Glory*. This manuscript was the last music score composed by William Henry Havergal, composed on his last conscious day, Saturday, April 16, 1870. The text by Dr. John S. B. Monsell is symbolic of the Trinity, having three lines in each verse, three verses in each section, and three sections for one hymn. This score was posthumously named "Havergal," and his daughter Frances Ridley Havergal wrote, "The tune with its serene melody and rich harmony is itself an epitome of his musical work" (*Specimen Glasses for the King's Minstrels* by Frances Ridley Havergal, London: Home Words Publishing Office, 1881), original book pages 109–110, page 765 of Volume II of the Havergal edition. See page iv of this book.

ILLUSTRATIONS

Note : Not all, but many or most of the illustration pages in this book were caused by the need to keep the same left-page and right-page orientation as the original books or scores. Though there are so many caused by this, these pages were needful or necessary, and twice as many pages could be filled with valuable illustrations.

An undated phtotgraph of Rev. Charles Busbridge Snepp. William Henry Havergal planned to provide music for a new hymnbook that Rev. Snepp was preparing to publish, but W.H.H.died on April 19, 1870, aged 77. After a short time, his daughter, Frances Ridley Havergal, took up the work and prepared very nearly all of the music for Songs for Grace and Glory, *a labor of love from 1870 to 1879. The music for S.G.G. was originally published as a Companion Volume of the music scores, entitled* Havergal's Psalmody and Century of Chants, *many or most of them composed by W.H.H. Later, both the music and the words were published together in a single volume, the "Musical Edition" of* Songs of Grace and Glory.

Havergal's Psalmody and Century of Chants is a true gold-mine of musical worship, true worship from God alone and unto Him alone, to His glory and the good of His people. Attention is called to the two pages of "Supplementary Remarks" by Frances Ridley Havergal (pages 163–164 of Volume V of the Havergal edition), who said better than these feeble comments the value of this treasure.

This facsimile reprint of H.P.C.C. is the Fourth Edition of 1877 published by James Nisbet & Co. Added to this Nisbet Fourth Edition, there are two groups of pages that are copied from the First Edition of 1871 published by Robert Cocks & Co.:

1. Just before the Nisbet edition begins (page 155 of Volume V, numbered Arabic 1 within brackets), the frontispiece, title page, and 23 pages (originally numbered in Roman numerals i–xxiii) are copied from the 1871 Cocks edition.

2. Immediately after the title page of "A Century of Chants" (page 403 of Volume V, numbered Arabic 249 within brackets), a set of 6 pages—four pages of "Prefatory Notes by W.H.H. and a two-page "Supplemental Note" on Dr. Crotch—are copied from the Cocks edition (numbered 249a to 249f within brackets).

These two sets of pages are the only pages copied from the Cocks 1871 First Edition. All the other pages of H.P.C.C. here are copied from the Nisbet 1877 Fourth Edition.

The Cocks edition pages i–xxiii have three sections: I. "Prefatory Remarks to Old Church Psalmody. 1847" by William Henry Havergal, numbered i to ix; II. "Prefatory Remarks to 'A Hundred Psalm & Hymn Tunes. 1859" by W.H.H., numbered x to xv; III. "Notes on Certain Tunes, (From Old Church Psalmody) 1847" by W.H.H., numbered xvi to xxiii.

The Nisbet 1877 Fourth Edition was unpaginated, and a need was felt to provide a numbering; thus the 21st century hand-numbering of pages was written by hand on photocopies, Arabic numbers within brackets, made by David Chalkley in 2002.

The researcher and editor asks of the reader patience, clemency, forbearance, in this surely imperfect presentation. As Charles Busbridge Snepp wrote in the first paragraph of his Preface to the definitive 1880 "New and Enlarged" edition of *Songs of Grace and Glory* (see page 525 of Volume V of the Havergal edition), the remarkably diligent, fine, invaluable musical editor, Dr. Glen Wegge, and I want to be able to say, within our very limited means and abilities, that "No pains or costs have been spared to make it as perfect and complete as our finite powers permit."

Laus Deo. Praise be to God.

    David Chalkley

Fourth Edition.

IN MEMORIAM.

HAVERGAL'S PSALMODY.

Being selections from 'Old Church Psalmody,' 'Hundred Tunes,' and unpublished manuscripts of the late Rev. W. H. HAVERGAL, M.A., Honorary Canon of Worcester. Edited by his Daughter, FRANCES RIDLEY HAVERGAL.

A. With full Prefaces and Portrait, .	6s. 6d.	
B. Do. without Century of Chants,	5s. 0d.	
D. Without Prefaces or Portrait, .	3s. 6d., 2s. 6d.	
E. Do. without Chants, . . .	3s. 0d., 2s. 3d.	
C and F. Chants alone, . . .	1s. 6d., 1s. 0d.	

ROBERT COCKS & CO., New Burlington Street, London, W. and through all Book and Musicsellers.

HAVERGAL'S PSALMODY contains the best results of the psalmodic labours of a lifetime in discovery, restoration, harmonization, and original composition. All well-known and valuable old tunes from English, Scotch, and German sources will be found in it, together with full supply for modern Hymns and Metres. There are 253 Tunes and 100 Chants, also Hymn Chants, Kyries, Glorias, etc. The Prefaces and Historical Notes are a treasury of information, and an armoury of defence of the principles of Church Music.

In the research for the Havergal edition, advertisement pages have been rich repositories of valuable details and quotations. This advertisement was found near the end of a copy of F.R.H.'s book The Four Happy Days, *a copy published by James Nisbet & Co. and dated 1874 on the title page.*

Havergal's Psalmody and Century of Chants was first published by Robert Cocks & Co., London, in 1871, with second and third editions by Cocks (third edition in 1872); James Nisbet & Co. (the primary publisher of works by Frances Ridley Havergal while she lived and after she died) published the fourth edition in 1877, and this is the definitive edition. F.R.H. added a few pieces she composed. This is a very important, valuable work.

This was called a "Companion Volume to *Songs of Grace and Glory*." S.G.G. was the most comprehensive hymnbook in the Church of England till that time: edited by Rev. Charles Busbridge Snepp (words) and F.R.H. (music), most of the music in S.G.G. was taken from *Havergal's Psalmody and Century of Chants*.

The full title is: *Havergal's Psalmody and Century of Chants from "Old Church Psalmody," "Hundred Tunes," & Unpublished Manuscripts of the Late Rev. W. H. Havergal, M.A., Honorary Canon of Worcester with Prefaces, Indices, and Portrait Edited by his daughter, Frances Ridley Havergal.* Rev. William Henry Havergal had published *Old Church Psalmody* in 1847 and *A Hundred Psalm and Hymn Tunes* in 1859. William Henry Havergal (1793–1870) was the foremost church musician and composer of sacred music in England in his generation, as Lowell Mason and other contemporaries would have confirmed. (Note: Dr. Crotch was in the previous generation, and William Sterndale Bennett was not primarily a church musician.) A leading reformer of church music, W.H.H. did much to raise the level of singing in worship services. A very gifted pianist and organist, he published over 50 compositions, for example *The Grand Chant in Forty Different Forms*, Opus 52, in 1867. His priority was to be a pastor, truly a heart business, and he sooner wanted to prepare sermons than to compose music, his music being a supporting part to his ministry. He concentrated on music—with rare, fine ability—only when his health precluded his pastoral ministry.

This next published article on William Henry Havergal was found among Havergal manuscripts and papers. This was almost certainly written by Andrew James Symington, because passages in this article are identical to another published article definitely written by Symington.

Biographical Sketch.
of
Rev. W. Havergal, A.M. Editor of "OLD CHURCH PSALMODY."

Note.—The following sketch of his friend's life, by the Editor of the present Supplement, is reprinted from *The Musical Amateur* for June 1861. To make clear an allusion to the previous notice of Gluck, a portion of the last sentence in the "sketch" of that master's life is here added:—" We may consider him as indeed a great musician, worthy the memorial the son of Sirach invites: 'Let us now praise famous men, such as found out musical tunes. There be of them that have left a name behind them, that their praises might be reported.' " *Ecclus.* xliv. 1, 5, 8.

HAVERGAL.

We closed the notice of Chevalier Gluck in our last number with a quotation from the book of *Ecclesiasticus*, which we considered peculiarly apt in reference to that gifted individual. Its aptitude we consider equally great, excepting in one particular, in regard to the subject of our present notice. In that one particular, however, we hope for a long time to be at fault, and many, we are sure, concur with us in that hope. But though we cannot say of the subject of our present notice that he is "of them that have left a name *behind* them," it is by all but universal consent that "his praises are reported" as a most learned Ecclesiastical Musician and the greatest Psalmodist of this generation.

Rev. William Henry Havergal, A.M., Incumbent of Shareshill, and Hon. Canon of Worcester, was born in the last decade of the last century, in Buckinghamshire. His public education commenced at Merchant Tailors' School, from whence so many "famous men" have emanated. His early tastes fluctuated between Medicine and Music. Making the acquaintance of Dr. Crotch, while on a visit to Oxford previous to entering the University, he was recommended by the Doctor, who approved the skill evinced in his early compositions, to graduate both in Arts and Music, as did subsequently the late Professor at Cambridge, Dr. T. A. Walmisley, and as has done still more recently, the present Professor of Oxford, Sir F. A. Gore Ouseley, Bart, and a few others. He did not, unfortunately, act upon the advice given, but, intending to enter the church, and being a member of St. Edmund Hall, graduated in Arts only, as Bachelor in 1815, as Master in 1819.

In 1816 he was ordained, but it was not until his second Curacy, in Gloucestershire, that his taste for musical composition (laid aside for a time to make place for other subjects of study) revived. The singular musical skill of his Parish Clerk, who had a considerable local celebrity, was the immediate provocative of this revival. After removing to the Rectory of Astley, in Worcestershire, a distressing and all but fatal accident disabled him from the severer duties in which he was engaged. During several years of clerical silence, the result of that accident, his studious and active mind found relief in Music, the taste for which had so happily returned. His first published composition was an anthem-like setting of *From Greenland's Icy Mountains* the proceeds of which, amounting to £160, were devoted to a Missionary Society. Other compositions rapidly followed, and their proceeds were always devoted in the same liberal spirit, to some charitable object. Considerable sums have been thus raised, and many, indifferent to the charms of musical notes, have doubtless oft-times been gladdened by cashing the same. Several of these earlier pieces have become popular, and all are characterized by great sweetness of melody and skill of construction. They never sustained an unfavorable criticism.

In 1836 appeared Op. 35, *An Evening Service in E-flat, and 100 Antiphonal Chants*. Of the *Evening Service* it may be said that it is one of the modern glories of cathedral music. Of the *100 Antiphonal Chants*, their writer, as time rolled on, and a more correct Ecclesiology prevailed, did not judge so favourably. In 1849, Mr. Havergal published an announcement to the effect that he was willing to devote nine-tenths of them to the fire, and after that halve the remainder. For ourselves we may say that the *Antiphonals* were greatly in advance of the parochial chants prevalent twenty-five years ago, and were, in common with all the works of our author, noted for their skillful and pleasing construction. One of them, a "*Recte et Retro*" Chant in C, (now commonly printed in D, and sometimes called "Worcester Chant,") is as widely known as the language, and, short though it be, possesses all the elements of musical immortality.

In the same year as the above (1836), the Gresham prize medal was adjudged to him for *An Evening Service in A*, Op.37. In 1841 a second medal was gained by an anthem *Give Thanks*, Op. 40, decidedly one of the best compositions of the kind in existence. Upon thus gaining two prizes, the umpires ruled that henceforth no candidate should receive more than two. Other Anthems and Services proceeded at various times from the pen of our author, who, we must never forget, was, with renewed strength, constantly and untiringly engaged in the arduous duties of a minister of religion.

But it is in the restoration of Metrical Psalmody to its original purity, that Mr. Havergal has rendered himself so illustrious, and for which he will be long justly venerated. He has certainly done more and to better purpose in this way than any living Musician. Those whose labours come nearest his in greatness will be the first to confirm this. From Dr. Crotch he caught the true idea on this subject, which has greatly developed in his hands. He first of all published a reprint of Ravenscroft's scarce work, *The Whole Booke of Psalmes*, in 1844. At the close of an elaborate preface of 21 pages, he there promises,—"It is the intention of the editor, as speedily as practicable, to publish a selection of the tunes, with the cantus and tenor inverted or of necessity altered, to suit our present mode of singing. To such selection will be added other tunes, principally for other metres ; but strictly in the same generic style of melody and harmony." This promise was redeemed in 1847 by the publication of *Old Church Psalmody*, Op. 43, of which most persons can speak as approvingly as ourselves. It is the best, and best principled book of Psalm tunes of which Protestantism can boast, representing as we believe, and as far as is now possible, the true ideal of the Reformation and its time. All compilers since 1847 have drawn largely upon the *Old Church Psalmody*. It is now in its fourth edition. In 1854 appeared a highly interesting volume, *A History of the Old Hundredth Psalm Tune, with Specimens*. In this it is proved, and as Bishop Wainwright in the Prefatory note says, "we think it will be generally conceded, that William Franc must hereafter be entitled to the credit of *composing* this most remarkable of all metrical tunes." The thanks of the archaeological as well as musical world are due to Mr. Havergal for this excellent History. In 1859 was published, *A Hundred Psalm and Hymn Tunes*, Op. 48, entirely of his own composition. This was due to his reputation acquired in this walk of Church music, for excepting in scattered publications by other compilers, no Psalm tunes of his own construction had been published. *The Old Church Psalmody* eschewed all modern compositions, as its name would lead readers to suppose. Its preface says:—"No composition of any living author is introduced." Of the *Hundred Tunes*, it is not too much to say that they are a monument of learning and industry; and are all, or nearly all, in entire agreement with the principles which so long and so successfully our author has propounded.

Handel, Corelli, and our great Cathedralists, are his masters. His aim is to preserve purity of style, and put down musical vanities. Notoriously liberal to publishers of music, he has been equally notorious in aiding, by scientific criticism and research, all who have applied to him. He has written and kept back far more than he has published. He is not a mere musician, but a theologian also, as his two volumes of sermons and other works of that class prove. These, as we know, are read with pleasure by persons widely differing from their writer's views.

In 1852 he all but lost his sight, which has been only partially restored. He is unable to read a note of printed music or decipher his own handwriting. Through weakened health, he has lately resigned a city Rectory (St. Nicholas, Worcester), and retired to the quiet of a small country parish. Long may he be spared to witness the growth of the principles he has so vigorously inculcated, and to receive the respect which all within his immediate influence so justly feel for him.

Note: This "Biographical Sketch" is unsigned, but the next piece, an article by Andrew James Symington, has passages which are identical, suggesting that Symington almost surely was the author also of this piece. This piece and the next article in the London *Morning Advertiser* have long passages that are identical also to the "Biographical Sketch" by Symington in *The Pastor Remembered and the Brethren Entreated.*

These next details about the origin of this book were given in the sterling biography *Records of the Life of the Rev. William Henry Havergal, M.A.* written by his daughter, Jane Miriam (Havergal) Crane (London: Home Words Publishing Office, 1882), original book pages 193–195, page 632 of Volume IV of the Havergal edition.

In November, 1847, my father published "Old Church Psalmody," a collection of old English tunes and others of foreign origin which he esteemed a desideratum, as he believed there was no existing volume which contained only such tunes and such harmonies as strictly accord with the style of those times when psalmody was best understood, and of which the date of T. Ravenscroft's Psalter, 1621, he considered the zenith. No composition of a later date which did not accord with that style was admitted, nor any tune by a living author.

"Old Church Psalmody" contained remarks on harmony, style, rhythmical form, the time and pitch in which the tunes were sung, followed by notes of information respecting many of them.[1]

He received numberless testimonies from America and Scotland, as well as England, of the high estimation in which this now standard work was held. It passed through five editions, and has since been incorporated with the next mentioned volumes. He published, in 1859, "A Hundred Psalm and Hymn Tunes," Op. 48. These tunes were selected from very many of his own composition, and are all constructed on the principles set forth in his "Old Church Psalmody." They are named from the natural geography of the Bible, as Amana, Bethany, Carmel, etc., a system which had not before been adopted, and is a distinctive mark of his later tunes. My sister Frances in like manner named her published tunes from the names of St. Paul's friends, as Claudia, Euodias, Hermas, etc. The preface to the "Hundred Psalm and Hymn Tunes" contains remarks on the secularities too prevalent in psalmody, etc., insisting that in music, as in architecture, the church should have a style of her own. In January, 1870, he published "A Century of Chants," with a preface, and a "Supplemental Note" on the career of Dr. Crotch.

When an Oxonian my father had the advantage of hearing Dr. Crotch on the organ in his best days, and of imbibing his musical ideas, for which he always retained the utmost veneration. In later years Dr. Crotch often expressed his high opinion of my father's compositions, and his respect for his judgment and learning.

In 1871, the year following his death, the above works were incorporated in one volume, entitled "Havergal's Psalmody," and published by his widow; but it was entirely prepared and arranged by his daughter Frances R. Havergal, with the addition of many of his other tunes, some kyries, and glorias, and also some of her own tunes, to which she afterwards added an appendix. Finally the Rev. C. B. Snepp published in 1875, by permission, another edition as a musical companion to his "Songs of Grace and Glory." This also my sister Frances arranged, adding new tunes by herself and other composers.

---

[1] In 1859, as in some other years, my father had much correspondence with the Rev. C. H. Davis, then of Nailsworth, who kindly gave him much assistance in preparing for the press one of the editions of " Old Church Psalmody," etc.

These next reviews (or excerpts of published reviews) of books were found in the advertisement pages at the back of a copy of *Under the Surface* by Frances Ridley Havergal, Third Edition, published in 1876 by James Nisbet & Co., London.

HAVERGAL'S PSALMODY.

HAVERGAL'S PSALMODY contains the best results of the Psalmodic labours of a life-time in discovery, restoration, harmonization, and original composition. All well-known and valuable old tunes from English, Scotch, and German sources will be found in it, together with full supply for modern hymns and metres. There are 253 Tunes and 100 Chants, also Hymn Chants, Kyries, Glorias, etc. The Prefaces and Historical Notes are a treasury of information, and an armoury of defence of the principles of Church Music.

"The work of one who had a single eye to elevate whatever he touched, and has in this been so eminently successful. . . . We cannot imagine any one without this volume who takes any interest in Church Music.—*Glasgow Daily Mail.*

"Mr. Havergal wrote with a loving, scholarly, zealous hand, and his contributions to our Church Music are distinguished by a learning, grace, and skill which few have been able to equal."—*Midland Counties Herald.*

"We do not know a better or more carefully arranged work."—*North British Mail.*

SONGS OF GRACE AND GLORY.
FOR PRIVATE, FAMILY, AND PUBLIC WORSHIP.
*Hymnal Treasures of the Church of Christ from the
4th to the 19th Century.*
Edited by REV. CHARLES B. SNEPP, LL.M., Vicar of
Perry Bar, near Birmingham.

Full Editions (1025 Hymns). Prices 1s to 10s.
Public Worship Editions (520 Hymns selected from Full Edition).
Prices 9d. to 3s. 6d.
"Songs of Grace and Glory" for Mission Services, etc. (29, 69,
130, or 200 Hymns). Prices .d. to 6d.
The Children's "Songs of Grace and Glory" (178 Hymns).
Prices 2d. to 6d.
The Musical Edition, with all the Hymns complete, including
Appendix. 3s. 6d. to 5s.
An Appendix of 69 Hymns, suited to the requirements of the
present day, may be had separately, or bound up with any of the
above.

"SONGS OF GRACE AND GLORY," to which Havergal's Psalmody forms "Companion Volume," contains 1025 Hymns, embracing every Scripture Doctrine, every Church Festival or special occasion, and every phase of Christian life and experience. Suitable tunes, with metres, authors, dates, and texts, and affixed to each hymn; a table of hymns for Sundays and holy-days, and six indices, facilitate use and reference. It claims to be the most comprehensive and complete Hymnal in the Church of England.

"It will be a text-book to me all my days."—Ira D. Sankey.

An undated photograph of William Henry Havergal, with his inscription, and a color portrait of him painted by Solomon Cole in 1845.

This was an earlier title page of H.P.C.C. in F.R.H.'s handwriting. The title was later changed to be Havergal's Psalmody and Century of Chants, from "Old Church Psalmody," "Hundred Tunes," and Unpublished Manuscripts of the Late Rev. W. H. Havergal, M.A., Honorary Canon of Worcester. See pages 3 and 31 of this book.

Faithfully y^s.
W: H: Havergal

For other views of the sculpture of W.H.H., see page 2028 of Volume V of the Havergal edition.

Havergal's Psalmody

and Century of Chants

FROM

"Old Church Psalmody".

"Hundred Tunes" & Unpublished Manuscripts

OF THE LATE

Rev. W. H. Havergal, M. A.

Honorary Canon of Worcester.

with Prefaces, Indices and Portrait.

Edited by his daughter, Frances Ridley Havergal.

LONDON,
Robert Cocks & Co. New Burlington Street.
By Special Appointment.
Music Publishers to her Majesty the Queen, H.R.H. the Prince of Wales.
and the Emperor Napoleon III.
MDCCCLXXI.

In the Robert Cocks 1871 First Edition, these 23 pages (numbered in Roman numerals i–xxiii) are found between the "Introduction" by C. A. Havergal and the "Supplementary Remarks. 1871." by F.R.H.

I.

𝕻𝖗𝖊𝖋𝖆𝖙𝖔𝖗𝖞 𝕽𝖊𝖒𝖆𝖗𝖐𝖘 𝖙𝖔 𝕺𝖑𝖉 𝕮𝖍𝖚𝖗𝖈𝖍 𝕻𝖘𝖆𝖑𝖒𝖔𝖉𝖞.
1847.

THE DISTINCTIVE CHARACTER OF OLD TUNES

Has long been out of common recollection. Simple and easy in their phrases, and always syllabic in their partition, the commonest ears and least cultivated voices could master them. But, simple and easy as they are, they never are vulgar, insipid, or boisterous. *Grave, but cheerful, dignified and chaste, they are admirably adapted to meet a great variety of language, and to foster a calm and earnest devotion.* One test of their excellence, and of their intrinsic fitness for Church use, is the fact, that, little as flippant and self-willed singers may like them, all persons of sober taste and devout feelings delight in them. Many individuals, too, who, from early initiation, have been accustomed to tunes of a more light and trashy character, gradually come to a right estimate of those which are opposed to that character.

The harmony to the old tunes was sometimes of the simplest sort. The first of the Common Metres in this volume,* a tune set by Thomas Tallis, is a beautiful instance of severe but pleasing simplicity. Generally speaking, however, the old harmonists were inclined to a little cleverness in counterpoint. While they studied simplicity for the congregation, they rather *aimed* at ingenious harmony for the choir.† But, whether simple or ingenious, their harmony retained the following characteristics: 1. *Tunefulness of progression in all the parts.* 2. *Contrariety, or obliquity of motion between the extreme parts.* 3. *Fulness of combination; fundamental chords being preferred to half chords.* 4. *Closeness, or fitting distribution of the parts as to relative distance.* 5. *Avoidance of certain chords and discords.* 6. *Frequent interchange of major and minor chords.*

* [No. 44 in " Havergal's Psalmody."]

† To say nothing of foreign composers, of whom Claude le Jeune was the most eminent for this species of harmony, the oldest English Psalter, yet known, contains truly remarkable specimens of the clever setting of Psalm Tunes. The Harmonized Psalter, published by John Day, 1563, and which perhaps was commonly called " Parson's Psalms," abounds with modest ingenuities. The version of the 44th Psalm, " Another of the same, by R. Brimle," is uncommonly beautiful. The close of it is a clever instance of writing " In Reports," *i. e., bringing back* some part of the tune, and turning it into a short fugue.

ii   *Prefatory Remarks to Old Church Psalmody.*

From extensive and careful observation, the Editor is confident in saying, that the *beau ideal* of psalmodic harmony used to be *tuneful progression of the parts*, or the so constructing those parts, especially the Cantus and Medius, that of themselves they would constitute melodies, and, as the phrase is, "sing well." Indeed, the older harmonists seem to have been more ambitious of this sort of pleasing progression than of any other excellence. It is clear that they sacrificed little proprieties in order to secure it. They thought less of fulness and closeness, and even of proper consecutives, than otherwise they might be supposed to think. Not that they were inattentive to them, but everything was made subservient to melodic progression.

Their next especial aim was the writing of extreme parts in contrary or oblique motion. Direct motion between those parts certainly is not common. For want of attention to this fact, some editors, by printing new or inverted parts to the *literal* Basses of old tunes, have made the original harmonists appear guilty of what they are most innocent. Those Basses, upon reference to original copies, will be found set, not to the Tune or Tenor only, but to the Cantus or Treble part above both it and the Medius, or Counter Tenor. Hence, although the Bass may often proceed in direct motion with the Tenor, as *an inner* part, it goes in contrary motion to the Cantus, as *the upper* part.

In the avoidance of certain chords and discords, few instances, as opposed to modern practice, are more remarkable than what pertains to the $\frac{6}{4}$, the $\frac{6}{3}$, and the minor seventh. The $\frac{6}{4}$ is never used; nor was it employed by either Handel or Corelli. (See page xi.) The $\frac{6}{4}$ followed by $\frac{5}{3}$ upon the dominant, before a final close, *in the major mode*, and where the sixth is the highest note, is not frequently met with. Other forms of that chord are common enough, but this one, now so usual, is not common. Indeed, the old harmonists took pains to avoid it; and some German harmonizers of old tunes adopt new methods of escaping it. Except as a passing note, on the unaccented part of the measure, a minor seventh on the dominant is of rare occurrence. The ears of our forefathers would have been sadly startled by the secularity of that seventh, as now frequently employed in modern Psalm Tunes, as also by the running of Bass and Treble *unduly* in thirds, or other "*similar* motion," by the introduction of, what of old was intolerable, consecutive *major* thirds between the extreme parts, and by the making the dominant in the Bass to *ascend* with the leading note in the Treble, to the tonic, which the old masters especially eschewed, except when absolutely unavoidable.

Among old tunes were many more in the minor mode than we now use. Nearly half the tunes in Ravenscroft's Psalter are minors. Double tunes, too, were far more numerous than they now are. Long and short metre single tunes, especially the former, were scarce. Trochaics are not to be found in the Church Psalters. Orlando Gibbons wrote two or three for George Wither's " Hymns and Songs of the Church ;" but we are obliged to search German Choral Books for any stock of *old* Trochaics.

The TIME and PITCH of tunes, in older days, were not exactly as they now are. Singers formerly sang with good speed. A dozen verses, reduced to six by a double tune, formed a very moderate portion for one occasion. The modern drawl, which makes four single verses quite long enough, was, most likely, occasioned by innovations upon the syllabic style, in the early part of the last century.* When crotchets, quavers, flourishing turns, and " part tunes," as they are called, found admission into Parish Choirs, a slowness of performance necessarily followed. · The introduction, also, of tunes in triple measure, where the accented semibreve or minim is divided into two slurred notes, (such as Abridge, Irish, Rockingham, Manchester, &c.) was fatal to the continuance of pure psalmody. All such tunes occasion a slow and languid utterance, and oblige an unwelcome curtailment of the original words. (See page xii.)

As to the pitch at which tunes were *sung*, some of the " Introductions to Singing," published in the last century, leave us in no doubt. They disclose the fact, that the keys, or scales, in which the tunes were set, were no criterion as to the pitch in which they were sung. They were mostly set in only two or three keys, to suit the convenience of the printer, as to leger lines, and accidental sharps or flats : but they were sung at any pitch which best suited the singers. Now that the organ has banished the pitch-pipe, it is very desirable that our organists should be able to transpose at sight, or that they should possess copies of the same tunes in two or more keys. Weather, temperature, health or power of particular singers, difference between morning and evening, character of words, and sundry minor circumstances, frequently render a change of key, higher or lower, very expedient.

But, in stating the distinctive character of old tunes, it would be an omission not to mention the constant practice of beginning and ending each strain with a full chord; and the almost constant use of the *Tierce de Picardie*, or major third, at every close in a minor mode ; † as well as, on the contrary, the utter abhorrence of everything *appoggiatural* in the melody. The old tunes contain no instance of that mawkish

---

* Dr. Watts complains of the slow method of singing in his day. He wished for more stanzas than " five or six," and " a greater speed of pronunciation," which would be more agreeable to the psalmody of the ancient churches.

† [In this edition the *Tierce de Picardie* has been generally omitted, as less accordant with modern use. As an instance of its retention see SPIRES, No. 29.]

hanging upon the sixth or fourth, which now so secularizes most modern tunes. They settle at once, in a firm and masculine style, on the fifth or third. Nor must one other distinctive feature be overlooked, though inconsiderable in its extent, and well nigh forgotten. In old psalmody, whenever a discord was used, it was sung *in suspension.* The note which formed the discord was sounded to its syllable in *preparation*, and *held* till it was resolved. Modern practice discards this elegant custom; chiefly, it is probable, because it involves some little syncopation to which ordinary singers are not trained. The custom is, however, retained in several tunes in this work (*e. g.*, Bristol), with as much attention to accentuation as circumstances allowed.

The peculiarities which have been enumerated may be advantageously revived and followed; but there are

OTHER PECULIARITIES,

which altered times forbid our following. The oldest tunes are remarkable for broken or syncopated rhythm. They are not commonly composed of notes of equal length, in corresponding position; but comprise semibreves and minims rather capriciously disposed. The tunes in the old Genevan Psalter are famous specimens of this sort of irregularity. Ravenscroft, in 1621, seems to have delighted in it; for he actually printed melodies with more rhythmical syncopations than even older copies contained. It was not till Playford's era, about 1670, that the old church-tunes began to be written with equalized notation.

Another peculiarity, which cannot be adopted in our present use of the old tunes, is the early custom of assigning the tunes themselves to Tenor voices, and setting, for Treble voices, a merely harmonic part above. The custom continued, in lingering use, till the latter part of the last century; but the present generation is hardly aware of its ever having existed. The origin of the custom may be attributed to the circumstances of the times. Coeval with the Reformation, psalm-singing became so general, that *thousands* of people singing together in massive *unison* was a common occurrence. To relieve the sternness and monotony of such singing, skilful musicians, even the best masters of the day, composed parts of the popular tunes in such manner as allowed them to be sung by all the people, without alteration or interruption, and yet with sufficient embellishment to please the lovers of harmony. The effect of such singing, as Bishop Jewel* describes, at Paul's Cross, and as

* Zurich Letters, Parker Society, vol. i., p. 77.

Prefatory Remarks to Old Church Psalmody.   v

Master Thomas Mace * descants upon, in York Minster, must have been magnificent and affecting beyond what any modern specimens can boast. This custom of composing ornamental, as well as essential parts, to plain tunes, was grateful to a choir, and encouraging to other singers. It allowed the congregation to sing what they well knew, and yet furnished variety to the choral body. For, as time advanced, the custom expanded ; and the same tune used to be set by sundry masters in sundry ways. Thus, by using old tunes in new dresses, the few became many.

THE CONSEQUENCES OF THESE EXCEPTIONS

are not inconsiderable. We cannot, conveniently at least, use the old tunes, in their earliest forms, either as to their melodies, or as to the manner in which they were harmonized. The melodies were subject to frequent alterations, both by editors and harmonists. Printers, too, in no trifling degree, originated or copied mistakes. In some instances, so great are the variations, that hardly two copies can be found to correspond. Hence, the utter uselessness of talking of original versions of old tunes. There are no such versions for certainty to be had ; and if we really had them, we most likely should decline using them. The origin of our old tunes is covered with the darkest obscurity. Indeed, that origin seems to have been disregarded. Excepting a few German tunes, nothing is known about the authorship of any. Consequently, we must explode the fallacy of reprinting old tunes with the names of certain old authors, as either the framers of the melody, or the composers of the harmony. The fallacious practice has, of late, become frequent. It is high time to denounce it.

It may be taken as an indisputable fact, that in earlier times little or no account was made of the authorship of the tunes themselves. What chiefly was regarded, was the *harmonizing* of the tunes ; or, as the phrase of the day expressed it, the "*composing them into parts;*"† for writers of the olden times used the term "*compose,*" in its Latin sense, not as meaning to make or frame a melody, but to "*put together*" certain parts which would harmonize with that melody. To all such labours the harmonists carefully put their names, and editors as carefully published

---

* Musick's Monument, pp. 18, 19.

† Oversight of this fact has occasioned a mass of error, in recent publications, which will not easily be removed. Editors, in their desire to give some information respecting the authorship of tunes, have superscribed the names of individuals, who, in a very different manner, *may* have harmonized those tunes, but who did not frame those tunes themselves. Tunes have, consequently, been assigned to Douland, Ravenscroft, and others, which were in existence before their birth.

vi   *Prefatory Remarks to Old Church Psalmody.*

them.*   But, as the same tune was harmonized by many individuals, it is idle to put to it the name of any one, as though he were the sole harmonist of that tune. Besides, if he were the sole harmonist, we can no longer use his harmony precisely as he arranged it. We are *obliged* to turn his Tenor into a Treble, and make corresponding alterations in the other parts. Our conclusion, therefore, is this :— Whoever undertakes to reharmonize old tunes, *must be independent of everything but their style.* That style has been lamentably neglected. The present work is an effort to restore it.

MODERN COLLECTIONS

of Psalm tunes differ greatly from old collections. The efforts of editors in the last century, and in the early part of the present, tended to discard what was old and good, and to introduce what was new and bad. These tendencies gradually increased. Until Dissenting bodies began to publish collections of tunes, the many local collections by country churchmen generally contained a majority of the old and good. But the plague of sing-song, glee-like productions then spread into almost every part of the Established Church.

It has long been complained that collections of tunes are too numerous. The real grievance is, they are too faulty. Some are vicious and injurious ; others, from the medley they contain, are of little value. Even the few which profess better taste, fall into incongruities, or afford dangerous precedents under hope of alluring to a higher standard. [*N.B.*—Written in 1847.] The chief fault of this class is not merely the introduction of questionable tunes, but the spoiling of good tunes by inconsistent harmonization. Modern harmonies are set to ancient melodies. The harmonies are such as were purposely avoided when the melodies were composed. This fault paves the way for, or perpetuates, other faults ; especially that of not preserving a distinction between what is secular and what is ecclesiastical in style.

THE INTENTION OF THE PRESENT WORK

is to supply a desideratum: for the editor is not aware of any volume which contains only such tunes and such harmonies as strictly accord with the style of

---

* " Honest John Playford" put his name to every psalm tune, new and old, in his folio of 1671 ; but he never imagined that he could be supposed to claim the authorship of the tunes themselves. *His* " Solemn Music" was the harmony "*On* the Common Tunes to the Psalms." Este and Ravenscroft had done the like long before.

those times, when psalmody seems to have been best understood. The date of Thomas Ravenscroft's Psalter, 1621, may be reckoned the zenith of those times.

In compiling "Old Church Psalmody," anxious attention has been paid to the rules and taste of the times alluded to. No composition of any living author is introduced; nor any of a later date, which does not accord with the style of an earlier age.

THE TUNES IN THIS VOLUME

have been selected with an eye to *utility*, and not to curiosity or learned excellence. Many a tune has been omitted, because, though heartily liked by the editor, it would not interest most persons. For this reason, he has not adopted more of the oldest tunes in double measure, and in a minor key. Those tunes are not lost.* They can easily be obtained; and where they are admired, ability will not be wanting to prepare them for use. Other tunes, also, are omitted, because of their similarity to some which have been inserted. So similar, indeed, are not a few old tunes, that the probability is, they are merely varied versions of certain originals. There are also, among psalmists, as among other classes of composers, certain *stock phrases*, which are regarded as common property. In the present selection, it has been impossible to avoid them. They would have been more numerous, but for the omissions alluded to. When they occur, or whenever part of a tune is repeated, old practice has been followed by harmonizing them in a varied manner.

For the harmony of the following tunes, with two exceptions only, (Tallis's Common Metre, and Alison's Winchester,) the editor is entirely responsible. In a few instances, and wherever he could, he has literally followed parts of certain tunes as harmonized by certain persons; but generally he has practised that independence which he has recommended to others.

THE RHYTHMICAL FORM,

which, out of many, the editor has adopted for most of the tunes, may be objected to; but it is generically the *old* form, the *traditional* form, and *the only one which all*

---

* Este's Collection, 1592, has been edited by Dr. Rimbault, for the Musical Antiquarian Society: and Ravenscroft's, 1621, by the editor of the present work. To the Preface of the latter publication, readers are referred for a fuller account of old tunes; also, to Hackett's "National Psalmist," and the Rev. J. Fawcett's "Lyra Ecclesiastica;" the Prefaces to which are by the writer of these remarks.

singers feel to be natural. To make the first and last note of every strain a semibreve, may appear somewhat untheoretical; but the appearance is confined to the music-paper, without any strangeness affecting the ear.

In addition to Mr. Hullah's *practical* and proper remarks upon the subject, (" The Psalter," p. xviii.) the following suggestions may still further " *tend* to settle difference of opinion." Old psalmists do not always assign a semibreve *to all* the parts *at once*, in the commencement of a strain. Frequently, the Bass sounds the fundamental note as a semibreve, and other parts follow a minim after. Hence, the commencement-notes may be regarded, as in Chants, the precursors, *ad libitum*, of the rest. They may be considered *variable* in their rhythmical use, affording liberty of extemporaneous adaptation to long or short syllables. Terminal notes are always allowed to be elastic, and why may not the initial ?

In measuring or *barring* the Trochaic tunes, the editor ventures to be singular; because he fully believes the universal practice to be wrong. Hitherto, Trochaic Tunes, when written with four minims in a bar, have been made to commence, in every strain, with a full bar. The consequence is, that the final note of every strain, instead of falling on what carries the *appearance* of the fully accented part of the bar, falls on the *seemingly* weaker division of it. By a very simple process, this common defect is now remedied. After all, it must be allowed that little exceptions may be made against even the best rhythmical arrangements ; for, whether we write tunes precisely as they should be sung, filling up spaces with rests, or occupying them with notes of entire quantity, or whether we depend on double bars, and allow conventional usage—there will probably remain some little hesitation on the minds of some persons. Good sense, however, and steady practice, will render all difficulties very little discernible.

CONCLUSION.

The old tunes of the Church of England ought not to be otherwise than interesting to every English churchman. If it be remarked, that in the present collection, there are many of German or Genevan derivation, it should be recollected that, between the old psalm tunes of England and the Continent, there is no essential difference. They have a common origin. Many even of our oldest psalter tunes were imported, by exiled Confessors, from Germany or Holland. The tunes of the Reformation, or of the age immediately following it, are like the doctrines of the Reformation—the same in character and tendency, whatever may be the quarter from whence they sprang. To have these tunes arranged for our use, will be accounted no mean privilege by those who value what should be the daily solace of our own hearts, and what cost many who sang them, their lives.

If, however, we would have these old tunes to perfection, we must attain more of the old fashioned piety with which they were formerly sung. Were it the motto of every choir, "*Let the word of Christ dwell in you richly in all wisdom,*" our congregations would more efficiently "teach and admonish one another, in psalms and hymns and spiritual songs." But, if music be substituted for religion, and singing for devotion, the best tunes and the best voices will neither increase religion nor aid devotion. It is much to be lamented, that *display* bears rule where it is most out of place. Few choirs are exempt from its withering influence; while it is generally found that those individuals who encourage it, by most indulging in it, are the first to give trouble by their conceit and self-will. A good, but humble-minded singer, is a singer of great value. By his good singing he may edify or encourage others; while, by his becoming modesty, he can hardly fail to check, in his companions, those risings of arrogance which spoil many a choir. Simple as the following remedy may appear, when proposed as a panacea for all the ills of all choral bodies in our parish churches, it nevertheless is confidently prescribed ;—When the minister or the clerk says, " Let us sing *to the praise and glory of God !*" let all the choir *in heart* say, AMEN !

" *The glorious Majesty of the* LORD *our* GOD *be upon us ! Prosper Thou the work of our hands upon us ; O prosper Thou our handy work !*"—Ps. xc. 17.

W. H. HAVERGAL.

St. Nicholas Rectory, Worcester.

First Edition .... Nov. 1847.
Second Edition...April, 1850.
Third Edition .... „ 1853.
Fourth Edition.. Feb., 1860.
Fifth Edition .... „ 1864.

II.
𝔓𝔯𝔢𝔣𝔞𝔱𝔬𝔯𝔶 𝔅𝔢𝔪𝔞𝔯𝔨𝔰 𝔱𝔬 "𝔄 𝔥𝔲𝔫𝔡𝔯𝔢𝔡 𝔓𝔰𝔞𝔩𝔪 & 𝔥𝔶𝔪𝔫 𝔗𝔲𝔫𝔢𝔰."
1859.

IN the year 1847, the Composer of these Tunes published his "OLD CHURCH PSALMODY."

The sale of that work fully realized the expectations of the publisher, to whom alone its pecuniary interest pertained.   No sort of effort was made to bring the work into notice.   Little more than a sovereign was expended in advertising it ; and no review was invited to recommend it.   Its circulation, nevertheless, has been very extensive, and its practical influence confessedly great.   Its editor takes no credit to himself for these facts, but gratefully attributes them to the growing readiness of thoughtful persons to acknowledge right principles and to follow correct taste, when brought out of the oblivion into which they had been so long cast.   Testimonies to this effect from America and Scotland; as well as from every part of England, have crowded the editor's desk.

Till the publication of "OLD CHURCH PSALMODY," including its Preface, the principles on which it was compiled had long been comparatively dormant.   By its circulation, however, those principles have been so far revived as to be generally acknowledged ; while most editors of subsequent compilations have either culled its contents or made them the basis of their own works.   Still it remains, as far as the editor knows, the only publication which fully and consistently adheres to that style of melody and harmony which is as classical as it is ecclesiastical, namely, the style of the Reformation age.   Long trial has proved it to be the best for popular use.   It is still the only style of the Protestant Churches of Germany, and the prevailing one in other parts of the Continent.*

To the statements and opinions advanced in the preface of the " OLD CHURCH PSALMODY," the writer of them most firmly adheres, because he believes them to be grounded on indisputable truth.   Upon a few points, however, about which inquiry has been made, it may be desirable at the present opportunity to offer some explanation.

* As a corroboration of what is here asserted respecting the Reformation style, the following extract is both opportune and interesting.   It is from " BISHOP COVERDALE'S FRUITFUL LESSONS," &c., (p. 471, Parker Society,) respecting "The Order of the Church in Denmark for the Lord's Supper :"— *" And at the quire door beside the table of the Lord, stand two good sober singing men, which (commonly a quarter of an hour afore the sermon,) begin a psalm; and all the people, both old and young, with one voice do sing with them, after such a fashion that every note answereth to a syllable, and every syllable to one note commonly, and no more, so that a man may well understand what they sing."*

Prefatory Remarks to "A Hundred Psalm and Hymn Tunes."   xi

I.—It has been asked, "*Why may not the chord of $\frac{6}{4}$ be used in psalmody, seeing that the greatest modern composers use it in their sacred music?*" The answer is—Such composers overlook certain facts :—1. That Handel, and all masters before him, sedulously avoided the chord,* as being inconsistent with the rule of the *discordant* character of the fourth, and the consequent necessity of its resolution. 2. That themselves habitually treat the fourth as a discord in all other combinations, and thus incur the charge of inconsistency. 3. That sheer *indolence* in facing a difficulty is often the evident reason of their condescending to use the chord. 4. That, as the use of $\frac{5}{3}$ instead of $\frac{6}{4}$ is one of the characteristics of the best age of psalmody (Ravenscroft, 1621) the disuse of the chord in question is requisite for keeping up the *purity* of psalmodic harmony.

II.—It has also been asked, "What sort of '*little proprieties*' are they which older harmonists were wont to '*sacrifice for the sake of a tuneful progression of the parts?*'"

They were chiefly of this sort : consecutive fifths and eighths by contrary motion, and even by direct motion, when that motion lay between the end of one strain and the beginning of another, or on the change of one mode or scale for some other. But of all the *essential* rules of counterpoint they were very observant. Certainly, however, they avoided that class of licenses by which discords of any kind, without regard to preparation or resolution, are even *studiously* introduced. This sort of licentious counterpoint is almost a characteristic, and assuredly the blemish and bane, of several well-intended tune-books of recent date. They originate, apparently, in their compilers failing to distinguish things which differ, such, for instance, as, that a psalm tune does not admit what a glee may invite, or in venturing to introduce *peculiar* harmonies, which have been met with in some modern oratorio or concerto.

III.—It has, further, been asked, "Can any *popular rule* be laid down for determining the 'greater speed,' or quicker time, recommended in the 'OLD CHURCH PSALMODY?'"

As a general rule, and in an ordinary congregation, a pendulum † of twenty inches will give, by each stroke right and left, about the fitting time for a minim. In tunes

---

* An extempore pendulum can be easily formed by the plainest performer. A piece of string or tape tied to a pocket-knife, or any such article, will furnish the instrument.

† "Mattheson (Orch. I., 1713, p. 128) rejects the fourth from among the concords and asserts its dissonant nature. Handel, Corelli, &c., have uniformly omitted it in the harmony of $\frac{6}{4}$. The theory of the one and the practice of the other seem to be, in this instance, justified by the want of melody in the intermediate parts, when the fourth is inserted."—*Dr. Callcott's Mus. Gram.*, *2nd Ed., p.* 172.

of triple time, Trochaic measure, or any sort of mixed measure, a line of fifteen inches will be expedient.

This rule, however, must be taken not absolutely, but elastically ; because massive congregations and resonant churches require a slower time than their opposites. Precentors, also, and organists, should devoutly study the character of the psalm or hymn to be sung, and regulate the time of the tune accordingly, especially if the tune be one of a solemn character.

The writer of these pages is well assured that his recommendation of a return to the speedier time of our Protestant forefathers has, in many places, been most beneficially followed. But he has reason to fear that, in some quarters, his recommendation has been carried beyond due bounds. Too great rapidity is as objectionable as too great slowness. The one is as liable to run into irreverence as the other is to sink into dulness. Devout consideration will always fix the true medium. (See page iii.)

IV.—As an apology for the continuance of modern secularities in melody and harmony, some *strange* things have been deliberately said to the Author of the present work.

1. It has been said that, " Such harmonies are more acceptable to modern ears, and more familiar to modern singers, especially unlearned singers."

That such harmonies are " more *familiar*" to modern ears is the only reason why they are " more *acceptable.*" Modern ears are, in too many instances, vitiated ears. They have been accustomed to trashy melodies and illiterate harmonies, or to adaptations of popular airs.* This accounts for their acceptableness, and, at the same time, furnishes a strong argument for their banishment. Progressing experience proves that, where the good in congregational psalmody is properly substituted for the bad, the former is heartily approved. If, however, by the language used, with regard to "*unlearned* singers," it is meant that modern harmonies are *more easy* to such singers, then the rejoinder must be—*This is a great mistake!* Taking the harmonies of the " OLD CHURCH PSALMODY " as essentially representing those of the Ravenscroftian age, it may be confidently asserted that they are more easy than those of many a modern publication, inasmuch as they are less "*stuffed* with discords," less chromatic, less extreme in pitch, and, what is of prime consequence, *far more tuneful,* and therefore, far more easy to be attained and retained by " unlearned singers." The Author has been repeatedly certified of the validity of

---

* On this topic abundant attestation may be found in Dr. Crotch's Lectures, pp. 77, 78, 81, 82.

these facts by competent precentors, and other teachers of choirs. On one occasion it was stated thus in a letter:—"The parts of the tunes seem like tunes themselves. Our men say they are so melodious that they can *whistle* them as they go home."

2. It has been said that "The rules of older harmonists can hardly be called exclusively ecclesiastical, inasmuch as they adopted precisely the same laws of harmony in the composition of their madrigals, and other secular productions."

It is, indeed, most true, that psalm-tunes and madrigals were harmonized on the same principles; but it is equally true that the principles themselves *originated* with the psalmodists, and not with the madrigalists. It is certain that the world *used* to borrow its style of music from the Church. This fact is no argument for the Church *now* to borrow her music from the altered style of the world. Because the world has waxed wild and wanton in musical taste, the Church has greater need sedulously to adhere to her own pure, sober, and decorous style of both melody and harmony. It is as becoming for her to have a musical style of her own * as it is for her to retain her peculiar dialect, dress, and architecture.

It may be added, as already adverted to, that the Ravenscroftian style, once so extremely popular, either constitutes, or very nearly approximates, the true *" via media"* between modern secularities † and those semi-barbarian antiques of "THE HYMNAL NOTED," which never were, and never can be, popular.

3. It has been said that "It was always an allowed practice to clothe older melodies, from time to time, in newer harmonies, according to the altered usages and tastes of the age."

Again it may be said, It is most true that such practice was allowed. But again, also, an omission must be supplied, because the circumstances under which the practice was allowed do not seem to be duly considered.

The allowance was made only within *consistent limitations*. The laws of harmony observed by Thomas Tallis‡ and William Parsons, differed in no essential principle

---

* " Church music has a proper character of its own, which is more excellent than that of secular or profane music, and *should always be preserved."—Rev. W. Jones, of Nayland.*

† It has recently been ascertained that the very popular tune, " Helmsley," so generally sung to " Lo! He comes, with clouds descending," is an adaptation from *Miss Catley's Hornpipe, in the " Golden Pippin,"* performed at Covent Garden Theatre, and published by Thompson in 1744. A copy from the original is in the possession of C. E. Stephens, Esq., Organist of the Parish Church of Hampstead, Middlesex.

‡ A tune in the key of G, of a rather sing-song sort, but containing a little double counterpoint, has been going the round of several recent publications, and assigned to Thomas Tallis. It has, at length, been proved to be merely an off-hand enlargement of an old chant, by a modern Organist of some talent. The Author is indebted for this fact to its indefatigable discoverer, and his worthy correspondent, Mr. J. C. Ward, Organist of Eaton Chapel.

xiv   *Prefatory Remarks to "A Hundred Psalm and Hymn Tunes."*

from those of Orlando Gibbons and Thomas Ravenscroft, three-quarters of a century later. The chief difference between the two sets of composers was, that the latter was more graceful and fluent than the former. For full a century afterwards, the system and style which Ravenscroft substantiated was paramount in all the parochial choirs of our land. * As fast as new composers, harmonists, and publishers of psalm tunes sprang up, the utmost homage was paid to the labours of "Master Thomas Ravenscroft."

Hence, so far as psalm tunes are concerned, no *such* clothing of old melodies with new harmonies was extant, as that which has been too common in recent days. Unless, therefore, some proper limit be defined, and some consistent stand be made, the practice in question will take some new start on the inclined plane of extravagance.

The tunes in the present volume are selected from a *much larger* number composed by the Author during a rather long series of years. Hence, as he has not been in haste with those now published, and is quite content to keep out of sight more than double their number, he trusts he will be pardoned by younger composers for venturing to give them a hint or two. Let them, then, adhere to the best models, and eschew everything which tends to vitiate ecclesiastical style. Let them not be tempted to copy what may seem *pretty* or *novel* in an oratorio or semi-sacred composition. Prettiness and novelty, as generally understood, are out of place in psalmody. When they have composed a few tunes, let them be slow to give them publicity, but most ready to submit them to the severest tests. Delay in such cases will save from many regrets, and prove the most stringent critic to have been the best friend. Above all, let them regard the composition of a church tune as " *a holy thing,*" seeing that it should be, as Jeremy Collier said, "fit for a martyr to sing and an angel to hear," and that it is intended to be the medium of the praise of many hearts at once before that Divine Mediator, who alone can render our music acceptable to the Triune God.

From what has been stated, it will be inferred, almost as a matter of course, that the tunes now published are framed after the model of those in the " OLD CHURCH PSALMODY." Such, indeed, has been the aim of the Composer, though it is proper to confess that the later, rather than the earlier models, have been chiefly followed. In accordance with the stand which is avowedly taken, *melodious progression* of the

* "It has been rightly observed that the music from the Reformation to the Restoration was more plain and solemn in its style than that which succeeded, though it still preserved great excellence."—*Rev. W. Jones, of Nayland.*

Prefatory Remarks to " A Hundred Psalm and Hymn Tunes."   xv

parts* has been studiously attempted. To further this desirable purpose, most of the tunes have been composed " on a subject," *i.e.*, some other part, besides the treble, but generally the bass, repeats the melodic phrase which characterizes the tune. This repetition is not always in the octave, but frequently in the fifth. Devices of this sort were formerly in much repute, but in psalmody they are of no practical value, unless they are really *pleasing*. The ear, and not the eye, must be the sole arbiter. In the instances at hand, no sign of the subject, or mark of its repetition, has been inserted. It may interest the student to discover *the idea*, while the unlearned singer or performer is neither the wiser nor the worse for it. Only, it may not be inopportune to remark, that some of the most artificial tunes in this volume have been decidedly the most popular.

To some of the shorter Trochaic measures a Hallelujah has been appended. In each instance it is so constructed as to be perfectly easy for the trebles and the congregation to sing ; and, in each instance, also, it is quite independent of the tune itself, and so may be adopted or omitted at pleasure. The use of a Hallelujah was common in the hymns of the early church ; its more frequent introduction now will be a beneficial practice.

The tunes are *barred* in the same manner as in the " OLD CHURCH PSALMODY," and for the same reasons as therein assigned. The stroke of a pen or pencil will be an easy method of alteration to those who desire it. (See pages vii, viii.)

The tunes are systematically named from the *Natural Geography* of the Bible. Mountains, hills, vallies, rivers, plains, and other geographical objects, often replete with poetry, are thus used for a musical nomenclature. As a *system*, this method of deriving names for psalm tunes does not seem to have been previously adopted. Happily, just names enough of a sufficiently euphonious character have been found for the present volume.

> * ———" No voice but well could join
> *Melodious part.* Such concord is in heaven."—*Paradise Lost.*

The Author may be allowed to add, that the composition of these tunes, and of the others alluded to, have been the recreative solace of many a valetudinarian hour, both at home and abroad. If in any degree they shall prove auxiliary to the glory of the Triune God, in the offering of congregational or domestic praise, the Author's first and highest object will be gained.

W. H. HAVERGAL.

Worcester, January, 1859.

b 2

III.

Notes on Certain Tunes.

(FROM OLD CHURCH PSALMODY.*)

1847.

No. 1.—THE OLD HUNDREDTH TUNE.

The authorship of this tune is more questionable than commonly is supposed. In England, it is confidently assigned to Luther. In Germany, no such confidence exists. Handel was of *opinion* that Luther composed the tune; but historical evidence does not support that opinion. Assigning the tune to Douland, or to any English author, is arrant folly. The editor hopes some day to throw a little light upon the subject.†

The present version gives the melody exactly as in Day's Psalter of 1563. The harmony is constructed partly from Parson's copy in that Psalter, and partly from the Herborne version of 1595. It avoids the formidable objection which hangs upon the common harmonization, viz., that with only one exception, each strain begins and ends with the tonal harmony. "Another of the same" is merely a consistent arrangement of the common monotonous version. The shape of the melody, however, is more ancient than sometimes is supposed. The harmony of the former version may be used to the rhythmical arrangement of the latter.

No. 13.—TALLIS'S CANON.

Tallis composed and set this as a Double Long Metre to a psalm, in Archbishop Parker's version (supposed about 1561). Ravenscroft, in 1621, reduced it to the measure of a single verse. It continued in common use, as a Morning Hymn, till the latter part of the last century; when, after various corruptions, it was printed and sung to Bishop Ken's Evening Hymn. The editor of John Wesley's "Foundery Collection of Tunes," in 1742, seems to have been the first person who published it in a corrupted form. In that collection it is called "Cannon Tune;" and is set to the well-known words, "Jesu, Thy blood and righteousness." The canon, which the tune contains, originally between the Tenor and Cantus, now between the Treble and Tenor, is quite lost sight of in all the corrupted versions. In transposing and arranging the canon, for the present work, care has been taken to avoid that constant repetition of the tonic and its harmony, which renders some recent arrangements rather monotonous. The tune, having no intermediate pauses, is well adapted for psalms or hymns of many verses.

No. 15.—OLD "TEN COMMANDMENTS' TUNE."

This tune is found in almost all foreign collections. The oldest version with which the editor has met, is in a beautiful Genevan Psalter of 1562. It is therein set to a metrical

* The notes in brackets are added by the editor of "Havergal's Psalmody."

† ["A History of the Old Hundredth Psalm Tune, with Specimens," by the Rev. W. H. Havergal, was published, in 1854, by Mason Brothers, New York, and Sampson Low & Son, London.]

Notes on Certain Tunes.   xvii

paraphrase of the Ten Commandments. As our old English Psalters set it to a similar paraphrase, it was called in after-days by the name it now bears; though "Audi Israel" was frequently prefixed to it, being the Latin of the first words of the paraphrase. Este, in 1592, set the tune, as harmonized by Alison, to a second version of the 125th Psalm; and Ravenscroft, in 1621, copied it; adding another harmonization of it, by himself, to the "Audi Israel." Playford, in 1671, set the tune in equalized notation to the same psalm; but appended a poetical paraphrase of the Ten Commandments, by Dr. Henry King, Bishop of Chichester, to be sung to the tune. From the constant publication of the tune, in all the older collections, it may be supposed to have been a special favourite. Rink has fugued it in his Organ School. Werner attributes the composition of the tune to John Baptista, 1560.

No. 21.—DORTMUND.

The editor has been urged to insert a properly harmonized copy of what has been called Tallis's L.M. Tune to the former version of the VENI CREATOR,* "Come, Holy Ghost, our souls inspire," in the Ordination Service. But the task is declined, because there is every reason to believe that the tune was *not* the production of Tallis. Not only is it abhorrent to his style and age, but the very words to which it is set were not published till full three-quarters of a century after his death.†

The earliest known copy of the tune is to be found in "Short Directions for the Performance of the Cathedral Service," A.D. 1664, by Mr. Edward Low, Organist of Christ Church, Oxford. It may be his own composition, although the style of it very much resembles that of his contemporary and neighbour, Dr. Benjamin Rogers.

Dr. Crotch published the Bass and Treble of the tune in 1803; but on what authority he ascribed it to Tallis, does not appear. The worthy Doctor omitted to give the inner parts, possibly because of their ineligible character. Not a trace of the tune is to be found in any other early quarter.

In the absence of any authentic tune suited to the words, the editor has inserted one which has been deemed likely to meet with approval; though of German origin,‡ it accords with the style of Tallis. The Trochaic Coda or Doxology is framed from the tune itself: which, independently of the "Veni Creator," may be used as an ordinary L.M.

No. 22.—CRETE.

A tune composed for the former Hymn in the English Ordinal. It is specially intended

---

* To what tune either version of the "Veni Creator" was formerly accustomed to be sung in Cathedrals, the editor has not been able to discover. Owing to the frequency of Ordinations in private chapels, music was probably omitted altogether. Of late years the most trashy *adaptations* have been used.

† Tallis died in 1585, and was buried at Greenwich. The words were first printed in the revised Prayer Book and Ordinal of about 1661-2.

‡ No apology is requisite for this, as Germany and Geneva furnished the foundation of our English psalmody. It is, however, too frequently forgotten that the harmonies in many German Choral Books are not vocal, but instrumental. It has been said that the "OLD CHURCH PSALMODY" "took the lead in opening up the German *tune-stores*, especially as to Trochaic measures."—*From "Supplementary Preface to* OLD CHURCH PSALMODY," *fifth edition.*

xviii   *Notes on Certain Tunes.*

for such antiphonal use in a·Cathedral as the Rubric directs.   When the Hymn is divided into three stanzas of six lines each, the former half of the tune may be repeated except in the last instance.   [It may be used as an ordinary L.M. tune.]

No. 29.—SPIRES, OR "LUTHER'S TURK AND POPE TUNE."

In many old Psalm-Tune Books, it is called "Serva nos, Domine," from the Latin of the first words of the Protestant Hymn, "Preserve us, Lord, by thy deare worde," by Robert Wisdom, published at the end of all our Old Versions of Psalms.   The tune is unquestionably Luther's ; and Robert Wisdom's Hymn is little more than a translation of Luther's words.

The Hymn and the tune were extremely popular with our forefathers.   The tune was never omitted in the old collections, and rarely in any till the close of the last century.   In Day's Psalter, 1563, is an elaborate harmonization of it, besides a plainer specimen.

No. 32.—SAXONY.

The solemnity of this choral is most touching.   For Passion-week or Good Friday, we have nothing superior to it.   Its origin, whether Protestant or Roman, is uncertain.

No. 44.—TALLIS.

This is simplicity itself.   Both the melody and the harmony are the progeny of our great Cathedralist.   He composed them for the Veni Creator, in Archbishop Parker's Psalter.   A child may sing the tune, while manly genius will admire it.

No. 45.—YORK.

Next to the Old Hundredth, this was once the most popular tune in England.   The Scotch, who claim it, call it "STILT."   There are three harmonized versions of it in Ravenscroft ; two by John Milton, the father of the poet ; and one by Simon Stubbs.   The present (inverted) version is made up of the best parts of the former two.

As this is the first of the tunes from the Scotch Psalters, it may be the fitting place to remark that all the so-called Scotch tunes are excellent ; but it by no means follows that, because they appear in the Scotch Psalters, they are of Scotch origin.

No. 46.—WINCHESTER.

This is copied entire from Alison.   Most of his settings being for instruments, are too high in the Medius for vocal use.   The third strain of this tune occurs in the Old 81st Psalm Tune, and is to be found in others of later date.   The fourth strain is another instance of stock phrase.

No. 52.—ST. ANN.

This is a deservedly admired tune, and quite in old style.   Bach published a fugue upon it ; or, as some say, on a choral like it.   The identity of the melody of the first strain with

Notes on Certain Tunes.   xix

that of Carisbrooke, by Henry Lawes, is only one of many instances in which composers, without breach of honesty, write the same passages. The modulation at the close of the third strain is often most unjustifiably changed for that of the dominant. Editors, too, fear to follow the worthy Doctor Croft, as he followed his predecessors, in commencing the first note of the fourth strain on the tonal *full* chord, because of consecutive fifths. *Such* fifths no old harmonist ever declined. The tune was called St. Ann, most likely because the Doctor was Organist of the Church of St. Ann, Westminster.*

No. 53.—ST. CHRYSOSTOM.

[A single specimen of a great number of tunes, composed in earlier life by the Rev. W. H. Havergal; which, though melodious and much liked, were excluded from his "Hundred Psalm and Hymn Tunes," because imperfectly accordant with the standards of riper years.]

No. 54.—EVAN.

[This tune, "the popularity of which in Scotland, America, and the Colonies is quite unprecedented," (see *Tonic Sol Fa Reporter*, May 15, 1870,) consists of the 1st, 2nd, 7th and 8th strains of, "O Thou dread Power," a sacred song by the Rev. W. H. Havergal, the melody being unaltered. "EVAN II.," No. 77, is the entire melody of the same song, harmonized by the author as a C.M.D. about the year 1867. The following note, written upon a copy of EVAN, given as autograph at the request of a friend, supplies his own account of its origin.]—

"'EVAN,' framed by Dr. Lowell Mason of New York, from a sacred song. 'O thou dread Power,' by W. H. Havergal, M.A., original air first published in 1847. The beautiful words of the sacred song were written by Burns for the family of Dr. Lawrie. The music to them is in triple time, and in the key of A flat. The tune 'Evan' comprises only part of the original melody. As the American arrangement was a sad estrangement, I have reconstructed the tune after a more correct form. Why it was called 'Evan' I know not. Still I do not approve the tune.

"LEAMINGTON, *March* 19th, 1870.   W. H. HAVERGAL."

No. 55.—LONDON NEW, or NEWTON.

A tune universally liked. Generally ascribed to Dr. Croft, but certainly composed long before he was born. Why Ravenscroft omitted it is hard to be conjectured. The Scotch version, the oldest known, gives the third strain in a different form. The one in this volume is now commonly sung in both England and Scotland. The Scotch lay fair claim to its composition. It was probably called "Newton" from Newtown, the appendage to "the *auld* toun o' Ayr."

No. 58.—ST. MATTHIAS.

Written by Orlando Gibbons, to Wither's hymn, for St. Matthias' Day. Playford printed a vitiated copy of it, and called it "Exeter."

No. 60.—ST. DAVID.

Ravenscroft's version of this tune is disagreeably *jumping*. Playford published the present modified version of it in 1671.

[* An earlier copy has subsequently been discovered by the Rev. H. Parr, in "Abraham Barber's Book of Psalm Tunes," 1686. It is there called "LEEDS," and attributed to Denby, 1680.]

XX   *Notes on Certain Tunes.*

No. 66.—BEDFORD.*

Another comparatively modern tune in good style. Its pleasanter melody completely cut out an older "Bedford Tune," in A minor. The oldest copy of this newer Bedford, which the editor can meet with, is in "The Psalm-singer's Magazine," 1729. It should be noticed that the melody, though in triple time, has no instance of a semibreve split into two slurred minims. That device is modern, and constitutes a species of melody which the old psalmodists *never* adopted.

No. 67.—FARRANT.

This is a compilation from the beautifully "serene" anthem, "Lord, for thy tender mercies' sake." With slight exceptions in the parts, the tune was compiled by the editor's worthy friend, Dr. Edward Hodges, whom England has lost, and New York has gained. [Died 1867.]

No. 70.—CHESTER.

Or, "A Prayer for the Queen's most excellent Majestie."

This, in Este's psalter, is harmonized by John Douland, and has been reprinted as his composition. But the tune itself is only a tune of that day, and was harmonized, also, by John Bennet, a contemporary of Douland, and one of the best madrigalists of the Elizabethan age. Ravenscroft calls it CHESTER.

No. 72.—DUNDEE.

Dundee is older than "Windsor," or "Eaton," as the name of this noble tune. The Scotch claim it as a national tune. BURNS believed it to be such. Another poet said of it, " Could I, when being carried to my grave, wake up just to hear what tune would be sung at it, I should like it to be 'Dundee,' or, as we call it, 'Windsor.'" Dr. Gauntlett considers it an adaptation of G. Kirby (16th century) from a Gregorian.

No. 73.—ST. MARY'S, or HACKNEY.

A general favourite, and with Mr. Horsley, "the *beau ideal* of a psalm tune," though its origin is unknown. Playford first printed it in common time. There is no reason why it may not be used in that time. Dr. Gauntlett questions the congruity of the former half of the melody of the third strain, and proposes an amendment. There is some room for the question, but the amendment is itself questionable.

No. 75.—OLD 81ST.

This oldest version of this most cheerful tune differs from all later versions, in beginning most of its strains with three minims. It is the earliest known specimen of our tunes in triple time. It is said, but without clear evidence, to be an Italian melody.

* [This tune has since been found in "A Book of Psalmody," by Matthew Wilkins, supposed date, 1699. During the last century, it was generally ascribed to W. Wheall, M.B., Organist of St. Paul's, Bedford, who died in 1745. It has also been attributed to H. Purcell. This information has been kindly supplied by the Rev. H. Parr.]

Notes on Certain Tunes.   **xxi**

No. 85.—ST. MICHAEL.

This fine old tune is older than marked; for it stands in Day's Psalter of 1563, to the 134th Psalm; but as a double tune, with another ending. The editor had not discovered its true antiquity, when he spoke of it in his preface to the reprint of Ravenscroft.

No. 93.—MARANO.

It is singular that the third strain of this exquisite tune should be a prominent phrase in Handel's beautiful song, "Shall I in Mamre's fertile plain." "LA SCALA SANTA," from which it is taken, is the production of a Venetian nobleman, who delighted in the "Psalms of Degrees." The English edition of his works was published in folio, by Godbid & Playford, A.D. 1681.

No. 94.—SOUTHWELL.

This beautifully simple tune used to be confidently ascribed, like "St. David" and others, to Ravenscroft. It was printed long prior to his day. It is a good specimen of a Psalm-tune framed on a subject. Singular to say, its subject is identically that of Tallis's exquisite motet, "Absterge Domine," in the Cantiones Sacræ, 1575.

No. 148.—GIBBONS.

This is genuine English, and one of the very few Trochaics which our English composers wrote. It is from "Wither's Hymns and Songs of the Church." The treble and bass are by Orlando Gibbons.

No. 163.—HAVERGAL.

[This tune, rich, sweet, and solemn, was the last note of its composer's earthly praise.* It was written at the request of a friend, before 8 A.M. on Easter Eve, April 16, 1870. In less than twenty-four hours from that time the stroke of apoplexy had fallen, from which he never returned to consciousness. At noon, on Tuesday, April 19, he passed away to join that "new song," to which his whole life had been a prelude.]

No. 202.—ESDRAELON.

[Adapted from "A Cradle Hymn," a sacred song, by the Rev. W. H. Havergal, published *cir.* 1840.]

No. 203.—SALZBURG.

This is a well-known "Tantum Ergo," in somewhat modern style. Without touching the melody, the editor has endeavoured, by older harmony, to better its style, or to make it less observable. Though attributed to Michael Haydn, it is perhaps, as the late Mr. Latrobe thought, of earlier date.

No. 208.—ALTORF, OR LUTHER'S HYMN.

In the first edition of this work, the Editor noticed the many variations of this tune, as printed both abroad and at home. Scarcely two copies are alike. He also noticed the

---

* [It was composed for Hymn No. IV., in "Songs of Grace and Glory," edited by Rev. C. B. Snepp, LL.M., Vicar of Perry Barr.]

ambiguity of its origin, according, at least, to the surmises of continental editors.   Recently, however, he has met with Winterfeld's Collection of the Spiritual Songs of Dr. Martin Luther, exquisitely printed, as a Jubilee Book, at Leipsic, 1840.   In that work the tune, *i.e.*, the melody alone, as now given in this volume, is, on apparently the best authority, assigned to Luther.   It is described as first printed in 1524, but composed in 1523.   Instead of being set to an Advent Hymn, or anything like "*Great God, what do I see and hear!*" it was arranged to a "Christian Song in praise of the Unspeakable Grace of God, and of the True Faith," while one-half of the tune itself is totally different from all the current versions of it.   Henceforth those versions must be regarded as spurious imitations of a beautiful original.   At the same time, there is no reason for calling it "Luther's Hymn," more than any other of his composition ; especially as the words which have been associated with it are in no respect his.   The original key is F.

No. 227.—ANGELS' SONG.

The editor is glad to be able to *settle* the authorship of this most ill-treated tune.   *It is, unquestionably, the production of Orlando Gibbons*, and was set by him in three different forms in George Wither's authorized volume.   It is called "Angels' Song," from the words of one hymn to which it was set.   All modern versions of it not only alter the melody, but the rhythm.   The editor gives the original Treble and Bass, for those are the only parts published by Gibbons, but avoids that mixed rhythm which puzzles modern singers.   By stopping at the end of the fourth strain, the tune, as in one instance by its author, forms a Long Metre.

No. 239.—HANOVER.

From a statement of Mr. Professor Taylor, in "The People's Music Book," it is pretty certain that this tune was composed by Dr. Croft.   It is tolerably clear that it is not Handel's.   As it has been so confidently attributed to him, it may be worth a line or two to dispel the illusion.   Handel did not arrive in England till the close of the year 1710, and then only for a brief visit ; whereas "HANOVER" was printed, in the Supplement to the "New Version of the Psalms,"* in 1708.   It is so unlikely, as to be utterly incredible, that Handel, who was *never* known in Germany to have composed a single choral, should have composed this one tune to English words in a non-German metre, and that it should have preceded his arrival in England by two years or more.   The tune is, consequently, in accordance with authentic tradition, ascribed, in this work, to our worthy countryman, Dr. Croft. The editor has heard the [late] Rev. G. S. Faber, Master of Sherborne Hospital, Durham, say that his venerable father believed the tune was composed by the Rev. John Chetham, whose fame as a psalmist, and whose publications in Yorkshire, began *early* in the last century.

---

* In a copy which the editor possesses, it is headed, "A New Tune to the 149th Psalm," &c., and is set in two parts only, in the key of B flat.   The Bass is evidently intended as a sort of second to the Treble, and not as one suitable in a composition of four parts.   This is the case with the tunes of Gibbons and the brothers Lawes.   Oversight of this fact has led to much harmonic evil.

Notes on Certain Tunes.   **xxiii**

Nos. 251 and 252.—"NUN DANKET ALLE GOTT," and "EIN' FESTE BURG IST UNSER GOTT."

[These well-known German Chorals, though not included in "Old Church Psalmody," nor harmonized by its editor, are appended to the present volume by the advice of a friend, in order to complete the supply of peculiar measures. No attempt has been made to "improve" these fine old melodies, and the harmonies are transcribed nearly verbatim from Adolph **Hesse's** "Choralbuch."]

No. 253.—ST. PAUL.

[By the same advice, this tune has been composed and added, at the last moment. Though it may seem out of place as regards the metrical arrangement of the work, it is well that *Havergal's Psalmody* should thus close with an ascription of praise to the KING OF KINGS AND LORD OF LORDS.

F. R. H.

Ascension Day, 1871.]

COMPANION VOLUME [1]

TO

SONGS

OF

GRACE AND GLORY.

[2]

Written impromptu 13th Decr 1869 at 9 P.M.

Softly the Dew in the evening descends
Cooling the sun baked ground's tegale
Flowers all fainting its feeds and defends

Ere the wind...
Sweet gentle dew drops...

This is part of a manuscript in William Henry Havergal's handwriting, near the end of his life. The rest of this single-page manuscript, and comments on this, are found on the next two pages, 157–158.

Note: This was a blank page in the original book.

[3]

HAVERGAL'S PSALMODY

AND

CENTURY OF CHANTS.

This is—on the left side—a newly typeset copy of William Henry Havergal's hymn "Softly the Dew," of which the manuscript is given on the surrounding pages 156 and 158. On the right side is the significantly different text that was published at the end of Chapter IV of *Starlight Through the Shadows* by F.R.H.

Softly the dew in the evening descends
    Cooling the sun heated ground and the gale
Flowerets all fainting its feeds and defends
    Ere the consumings of mid day prevail.
Sweet gentle dew drops, how mystic your fall!
Wisdom and mercy float down in you all.

Softer and sweeter by far is that Dew,
    Which from the Fountain of Comfort is shed;
When the worn heart feels itself made anew;
    And its old pleasures are proved to be dead.
Lord, let Thy Spirit bedew my dry fleece;
I will then follow Thee, strong in Thy peace!

Softly the dew in the evening descends,
    Cooling the sun-heated ground and the gale;
Flow'rets all fainting it soothingly tends,
    Ere the consumings of mid-day prevail.
Sweet gentle dew drops, how mystic your fall,
Wisdom and mercy float down in you all.

Softer and sweeter by far is that Dew
    Which from the Fountain of Comfort distils,
When the worn heart is created anew,
    And hallowed pleasure its emptiness fills.
Lord, let Thy Spirit be-dew my dry fleece!
Faith then shall triumph, and trouble shall cease.

(Rev. W. H. Havergal: last hymn, 1870.)

[manuscript in W.H.H.'s handwriting, dated 13ᵗʰ Decʳ 1869 at 9 P.M.]

[the different text of this hymn, quoted at the end of Chapter IV of *Starlight Through the Shadows* by F.R.H.] "I will be as the dew unto Israel."—Hosea 14:5.

[4]

[handwritten manuscript, rotated on the page:]

Sweet gentle dew drops, how mystic your fall!
Bidding sorrow's flush disdain in you all.

Suffer sweetly for is shut Dews
Which from the fountain of comfort is shed
When the worn heart feels itself more anew
And its old pleasures are found to be dead

Lord, let thy Spirit even my dry fleece;
I will [HUSH] Abia bless thee, strong in thy peace!

Leamington.

This is the rest of the single-page manuscript in William Henry Havergal's handwriting, the first—top—part given two pages before this, on page 156. Frances Ridley Havergal, at the end of Chapter IV of her last, unfinished book *Starlight Through the Shadows,* quoted a different text of this two-stanza hymn, and she wrote at the end, "Rev. W. H. Havergal: last hymn, 1870." See page 520 of Volume II of the Havergal edition. Frances also quoted this hymn—in yet another different text—for the month of June in her *Red Letter Days* (see page 941 of Volume I of this edition). Note that his eldest child Miriam wrote in Chapter VII ("Hymns by the Rev. W. H. Havergal") of her biography *Records of the Life of the Rev. William Henry Havergal, M.A.* that the very brief five-line hymn "Messiah, Redeemer!" was the last he composed (see page 625 of Volume IV of this edition, and pages 1855–1858 of Volume V of the Havergal edition). The music he assigned to this hymn is found on pages 1848–1849 of Volume V (his manuscript score and then a newly typeset copy of "Pussy cat"). See also the definitive score entitled "Gentle Dew" on pages 1521–1525 of Volume V, slightly different from the score for "Pussey cat."

Note: This was another blank page in the original book.

HAVERGAL'S PSALMODY:

AND   [5]

Century of Chants,

FROM

"OLD CHURCH PSALMODY," "HUNDRED TUNES,"

AND

UNPUBLISHED MANUSCRIPTS

OF THE LATE

REV. W. H. HAVERGAL, M A.,

Honorary Canon of Worcester,

EDITED BY HIS DAUGHTER,

FRANCES RIDLEY HAVERGAL.

FOURTH EDITION.

London:

JAMES NISBET AND CO., 21, BERNERS STREET, W.

1877.

[6]

TO

THE BELOVED, HONOURED, AND CHERISHED

MEMORY OF

W. H. HAVERGAL,

WHO, WHILE ON EARTH,

PRAISED THE LORD,

AND NOW

In Heaben sings the Song of the Redeemed,

THIS VOLUME

IS AFFECTIONATELY DEDICATED

BY HIS WIDOW,

C. A. H.

INTRODUCTION. [7]

———•———

IN issuing the present volume, at the urgent request of friends, I desire to do some measure of justice to the memory of my beloved and lamented husband, whose labours in the cause of Holy Psalmody befitted the reverence due to the Praises of God, and the needs of His Church on earth.

The object aimed at throughout this work is to comprise, in a careful selection, such a number of tunes, varied in character and measure, as shall best serve for congregational edification and general use. To these are added Hymn Chants, Kyries, and Glorias, and a Te Deum Service, chiefly as specimens of what was approved by the Composer.

Those tunes now first published are taken from manuscripts, jotted down as composed, without revision or, as I believe, thought of publication. The entire arrangement and preparation has devolved on his youngest daughter, to whom the earnest endeavour faithfully to follow her revered father's strict principles and high standard of Church Music has been a delightful employment and labour of love. The friendly advice of the Rev. Sir F. Ouseley, Bart., respecting a few tunes, was requested and most kindly given, for which I beg to offer my sincere thanks. Also to T. Kilner, Esq., and other friends, for general interest in the work.

With unfeigned humility, as unworthy of being even instrumental in presenting the sweet strains of my gifted husband to the Church, I now offer them, with the prayer, that all who use them here below may one day unite with the sainted Composer in singing the everlasting melodies of heaven!

C. A. HAVERGAL.

LEAMINGTON, *May*, 1871.

[8]

HAVERGAL'S PSALMODY.

Being Selections from "Old Church Psalmody," "Hundred Tunes,"
and Unpublished Manuscripts of the late Rev. W. H. HAVERGAL,
M.A., Honorary Canon of Worcester.   Edited by his Daughter,
FRANCES RIDLEY HAVERGAL.

A. With Full Prefaces and Portrait, 6s. 6d
B. Ditto, without Century of Chants, 5s.
D. Without Prefaces or Portrait, 3s. 6d.
E. Without Chants, 3s., 2s. 3d.
C and F. Chants alone, 1s. 6d., 1s.

HAVERGAL'S PSALMODY contains the best results of the
Psalmodic labours of a lifetime, in discovery, restoration, harmonization, and original composition.   All well-known and valuable old tunes
from English, Scotch, and German sources will be found in it, together
with full supply for modern hymns and metres.   There are 253 Tunes
and 100 Chants, also Hymn Chants, Kyries, Glorias, etc.   The Prefaces
and Historical Notes are a treasury of information, and an armoury of
defence of the principles of Church Music.

Fcap. 4to ; 6s., cloth extra, red edges.

SONGS OF GRACE AND GLORY.
MUSICAL EDITION.

EDITED BY THE LATE
FRANCES RIDLEY HAVERGAL
AND
REV. CHARLES B. SNEPP, VICAR OF PERRY BARR
Full Edition of 1100 *Hymns with Tunes.*

LONDON : JAMES NISBET & CO., 21, BERNERS STREET.

This advertisement was found near the end of a copy of Memorials of Frances Ridley Havergal *published by James Nisbet & Co., with "Eigh-teenth Thousand" printing number on the title page (likely printed in 1880). Robert Cocks & Co. published the first edition of* Havergal's Psalmody and Century of Chants *in 1871, and later Cocks published a second and a third edition (the third edition in 1872). James Nisbet published a fourth edition of H.P.C.C. in 1877. The "Companion Volume"* Songs of Grace and Glory *was first published by William Hunt & Co. in 1872, 1,025 hymns, words only. In 1876 Nisbet published a "Musical Edition" of S.G.G. with the words and music for each hymn together. The definitively finalized "New and Enlarged Edition" of S.G.G. was published by Nisbet in early 1880, approximately six months after F.R.H. died (June 3, 1879) and six months before Rev. Snepp died (June 23, 1880).*

Note : This was another blank page in the original book.

IV.

𝕾upplementary 𝕽emarks.

1871.

MANY will be surprised at the large number of well-known and favourite tunes in *Havergal's Psalmody*. The fact is, that *Havergal's Old Church Psalmody* has been the fountain from which editors of subsequent collections have drawn—either at first or second hand—and the original guide to many valuable tune-sources, both English and foreign. It was the Columbus of tune-books; the pioneer, not to a New, but to an Old World of musical treasure. *Now*, the route is open and easy.

The retiring and unselfish spirit of its editor, as well as his devotion to yet higher work, prevented that assertion of its true position before the multitude, which has always been accorded to it by the highest musical authorities. "Little more than a sovereign was expended in advertising it;" and only once did he pen a remark upon any unfair treatment of his work. "To the multitudinous applications for permission to reprint tunes from the *Old Church Psalmody* no refusal was ever given, nor was any remuneration named. But the permission, when granted, has not always been duly acknowledged. Some tunes have been properly acknowledged; but others, taken *wholly* or chiefly from the same source, have been printed as though they belonged to the editor of the collection in which they appear. These oversights, which ought not to be made, have too frequently occurred." Also,—"It was due to *Old Church Psalmody* that they who were allowed to borrow its tunes, should likewise have adopted its names."

The selections from "*A Hundred Psalm and Hymn Tunes, by the Rev. W. H. Havergal*," will be found, as experience has proved them to be, easily learnt, greatly liked, and practically adapted for congregational singing. Of one of these, Dr. Lowell Mason, the great American promoter of choral singing, wrote as follows:—"I have lately introduced into my choir, and sung with admirable effect, your tune, 'ST. NICHOLAS' [now called 'EDEN,' No. 38 in this volume]. The effect of it was truly magnificent. My choir consists of about sixty singers; the different parts are well sustained, and about equally balanced. I have never heard anything come nearer to my *beau ideal* of Church Music than did the singing of this tune, on a fine Sabbath morning, in a church filled with people. It made a deep impression; and the next day, one and another was asking, 'What tune did you sing yesterday morning?' 'Where did you get that tune?' &c. The performance of 'St. Nicholas' [Eden] makes one feel as did Jacob at Luz, and involuntarily exclaim, 'This is none other but the house of God, and this is the gate of heaven.' Wonderful would be the effect of the Psalmody were all the people to unite in such lofty and majestic strains."—April 30, 1847.

In order to meet the increasing proportion of "peculiar measures," a number of tunes have been adapted from the Rev. W. H. Havergal's own melodies, (chiefly from unpublished MSS.), while, for extra measures which could not be thus supplied, a few tunes have been added by another hand. The present volume, therefore, contains tunes for all measures in the best modern hymnals. It is, however, specially adapted to the new hymnal, *Songs of Grace and Glory*, with its 1,000 carefully selected hymns, edited by the Rev. C. B. Snepp, to whom the editor of *Havergal's Psalmody* is greatly indebted for much kind counsel in the work.

Any clergyman or organist will be willingly supplied with a Tuneal Key for whatever hymnal he may wish to use in connection with *Havergal's Psalmody.*

The arrangement of the tunes is strictly metrical. After the regular L.M.'s, C.M.'s, and S.M.'s, the P.M.'s follow *in order of length of measure,* beginning with 5555, and ending with 12 10.* When several tunes belong to one measure, they are carefully arranged *in order of character,* beginning with the jubilant, and shading gradually to the plaintive, so that if an alternative tune for any hymn be desired, it will never be far to seek.

The nomenclature of *Havergal's Psalmody* is systematic. The *name* of each tune at once supplies information as to its origin. Old English, Scotch or German tunes, bear respectively English, Scotch or German names; those by the Rev. W. H. Havergal are named (with a few exceptions), from the natural geography of the Bible; the added tunes are named from "the friends of St. Paul." No departure from these rules has been made without some necessitating reason.

Amens have been appended for optional use, wherever such a close is not unsuitable to the "suitable words."

May this memorial, to one "whose works do follow" him, be to the glory of his God, who has now "made him most blessed for ever."

F. R. HAVERGAL.

* (N.B.—15 15. 15 15, will be found under 87, 87 D.)

[II]

A CENTURY OF CHANTS

(Sixty Single and Forty Double)

BY

THE REV. W. H. HAVERGAL, M.A.

HONORARY CANON OF WORCESTER.

Note: This page was apparently a mistake at this point in the book. This page has been left here, and also repeated where it apparently really belonged, on page [249] (page 403 of Volume V of the Havergal edition). David Chalkley

[12]

I gave my life for thee:
What hast thou given for me?

―――――

Frances Ridley Havergal
June 23. 1874.

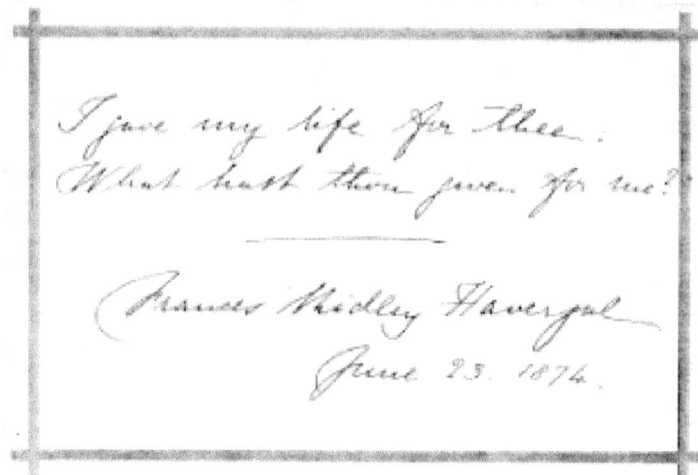

This was written by F.R.H.'s hand, and was printed (whether in a periodical, book, or on cards, is not known now), found among Havergal manuscripts and papers. See pages 2430–2432 of Volume V of the Havegal edition. This is hymn number 633 in Songs of Grace and Glory, *on page 801, and the score "Baca" written by W.H.H. for this hymn is number 116 in* Havergal's Psalmody and Century of Chants, *on page 239 of Volume V.*

Note: This was another blank page in the original book.

No. 1.   **The Old Hundredth Tune.**   (L.M.)   [13]

(See Preface, p. xvi.)

OLD CHURCH PSALMODY.

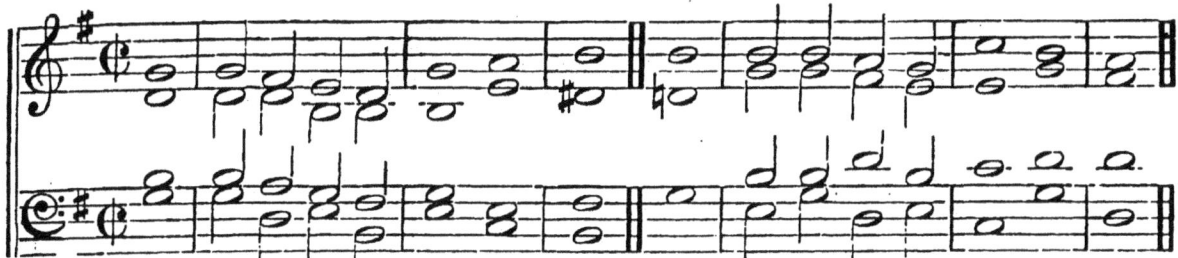

All peo-ple that on earth do dwell, Sing to the Lord with cheer-ful voice;

Him serve with mirth, His praise forth tell, Come ye be-fore Him and re - joice. A-men.

Another of the same.   (L.M.)

OLD CHURCH PSALMODY.

Be - fore Je - ho-vah's aw - ful throne, Ye nations, bow with sa - cred joy;

Know that the Lord is God a - lone, He can cre - ate and He de - stroy. A - men.

A

No. 2.   **Euphrates.** (L.M.)   [14]

W. H. H., 1848.

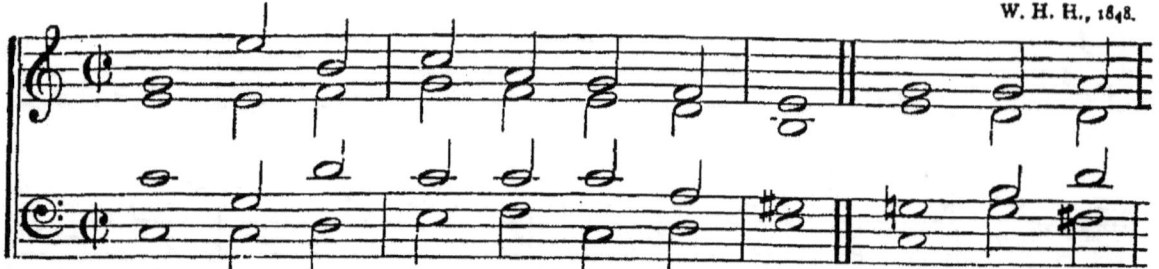

What are those soul-re-viv-ing strains, Which e-cho

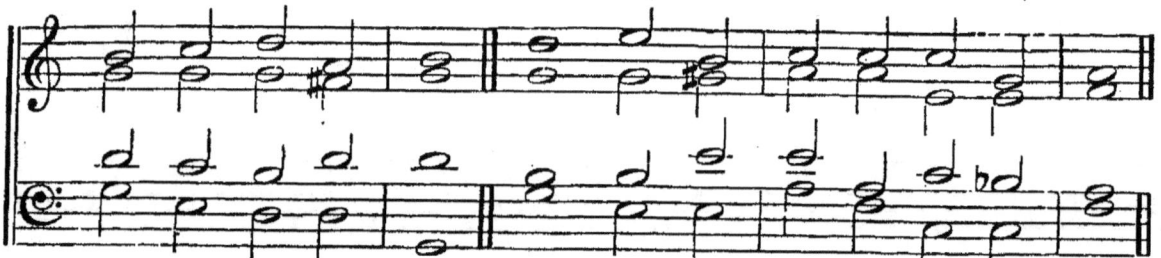

thus from Sa-lem's plains? What an-thems loud, and loud-er still,

So sweet-ly sound from Zi-on's hill? Ho-san-na! Ho-

san-na! Ho-san-na! A-men, A-men.

[15]

No. 3.   Crasselius; OR, Winchester New.   (L.M.)

OLD CHURCH PSALMODY.

The Sa-viour lives, no more to die; He lives, the Lord en-thron'd on high;

He lives, tri - um-phant o'er the grave; He lives, e - ter-nal - ly to save. A - men.

No. 4.   Waldeck.   (L.M.)

OLD CHURCH PSALMODY.

O ren - der thanks to God a - bove, The foun-tain of e - ter - nal love;

Whose mer -cy firm through a - ges past Has stood, and shall for e - ver last. A - men.

No. 5. **Wells.** (L.M.) [16]

Harmonized by W. H. H., 1860.

Soon may the last glad song a - rise Through all the mil-lions of the skies,

That song of triumph which re - cords That all the earth is now the Lord's. A-men.

No. 6. **Eppendorf.** (L.M.)

OLD CHURCH PSALMODY.

A - wake, my soul, in joy - ful lays, And sing thy great Re-deem - er's praise:

He just - ly claims a song from me, His lov - ing-kindness, oh how free! A - men.

[17]

No. 7.   Göldel.   (L.M.)
                                                    OLD CHURCH PSALMODY.

All hail, a - dor - ed Tri - ni - ty! All hail, e - ter - nal U - ni - ty!

O God the Fa-ther, God the Son, And God the Spi-rit, e - ver One. A - men.

No. 8.   Erfurt.*   (L.M.)
                                                    OLD CHURCH PSALMODY.

Je - sus shall reign wher-e'er the   sun Doth his suc - ces-sive jour-neys   run ;

His kingdom stretch from shore to shore, Till moons shall wax and wane no   more.   A-men.

No. 9. **Ḥaran; or, Bertram. (L.M.)** [18]

W. H. H., 1861.

O Spi - rit of the liv - ing God, In all the ful - ness of Thy grace,

Wher-e'er the foot of man hath trod, De-scend on our a - pos-tate race. A-men.

No. 10. **Gerar (Valley of). L.M.**

W. H. H., 1856.

O praise the Lord in that blest place, From whence His good-ness large - ly flows,

Praise Him in heav'n, where He His face Unveil'd in per - fect glo - ry shows. A-men

No. 11.   **Gilboa** (*Mount*).   (L.M.)   [19]

W. H. H., 1840.

Cap - tain of Thine en - list - ed host, Dis-play Thy glo-rious ban-ner high;

The summons send from coast to coast. And call a num'rous ar - my nigh. A-men.

No. 12.   **Hebron.**   (L.M.)

W. H. H., 1852.

I know that my Re-deem-er lives: What com-fort this sweet sen-tence gives!

He lives, He lives, who once was dead, He lives, my e-ver-last-ing Head. A-men.

No. 13.   **Tallis's Canon.**   (L.M.)   [20]

(See *Preface*, p. xvi.)   (Two in one, Treble and Tenor.)

OLD CHURCH PSALMODY,

Glo - ry   to   Thee, my God, this   night, For   all   the   bless-ings   of   the

light; Keep me, oh keep me, King of kings, Be-neath Thine own al-migh-ty   wings. Amen.

No. 14.   **Selnecker.**   (L.M.)

OLD CHURCH PSALMODY

O King of kings, Thy blessing   shed   On   our a - noint - ed Sovereign's head;

And, looking from Thy ho - ly heaven, Pro- tect the crown Thy-self hast   given. A-men.

No. 15.   [21]
Old "Ten Commandments' Tune;"* OR, COMMANDMENTS.   (L.M.)
(See Preface, p. xvi.)

OLD CHURCH PSALMODY.

God is the re·fuge of His saints, When storms of sharp dis-tress in - vade ;

Ere we can of - fer our com-plaints, Be-hold Him present with His aid. A-men.

No. 16.   Hor (MOUNT).   (L.M.)

W. H. H.

New ev'·ry morn-ing is the love Our wak'ning and up - ris - ing prove ;

Through sleep and dark-ness safe - ly brought, Restored to life, and power, and thought. A-men.

* Wrongly called ST. MARK, or MAGDEBURG, or ELY.

No. 17.   **Gennesaret.**   (L.M.)

W. H. H., 1844.

[22]

Let me be with Thee where Thou art, My Sa-viour, my e-ter-nal rest!

Then on-ly will this long-ing heart Be ful-ly and for e-ver blest. A-men.

No. 18.   **Bavaria.**   (L.M.)

OLD CHURCH PSALMODY.

Fa-ther of heav'n! whose love pro-found A ran-som for our souls hath found,

Be-fore Thy throne we sin-ners bend: To us Thy pard-'ning love ex-tend. A-men.

No. 19.   **Leipsic.*** (L.M.)   [23]

OLD CHURCH PSALMODY.

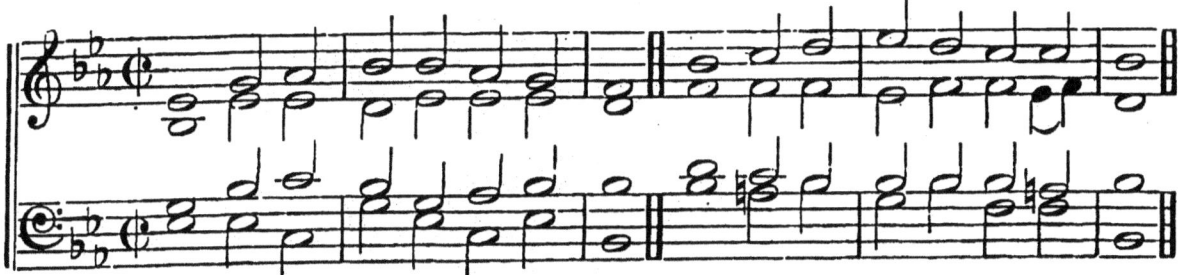

Take up thy cross, the Saviour said, If thou wouldst my dis-ci-ple be;

De-ny thy-self, the world for-sake, And humbly, meek-ly fol-low me. A-men.

No. 20.   **Dalmatia.** (L.M.)

W. H. H., 1859.

Come, gra-cious Spi-rit, heav'n-ly Dove, With light and com-fort from a-bove;

Be Thou our Guardian, Thou our Guide, O'er ev'-ry thought and step pre-side. A-men.

* **Wrongly called FREIBURG.**

No. 21. **Dortmund.** (L.M.) (VENI CREATOR.) [24]

(See Preface, p. xvii.)

OLD CHURCH PSALMODY.

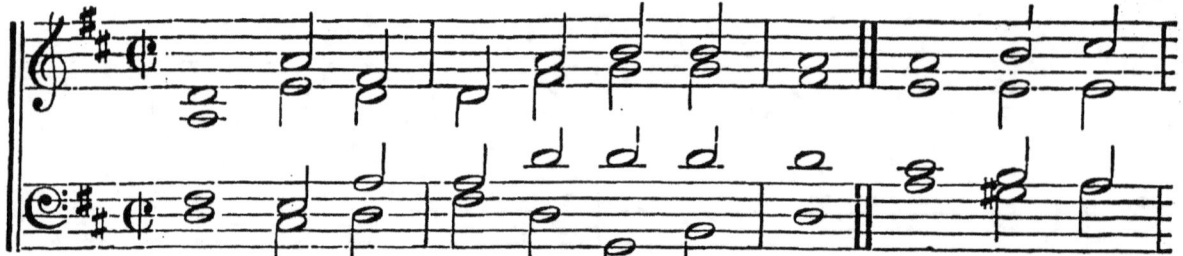

Come, Ho - ly Ghost, our souls in - spire, And light - en

with ce - les - tial fire: Thou the a - noint - ing Spi - rit art,

Who dost Thy seven - fold gifts im - - part.

TROCHAIC DOXOLOGY.

I raise to Thy e - ter - nal me - rit, Fa - ther, Son, and Ho - ly Spi - rit. A - men.

No. 22.　　　Crete.　(L.M.) (Veni Creator.)　　　[25]
(*See Preface, p.* xvii.)　　　　　　　　W. H. H., 1859.

Come, Ho - ly Ghost, our souls in - spire, *And light - en*

with ce - les - tial fire: Thou the a - noint - ing Spi - rit art,

Who dost Thy seven - fold gifts im - - part.

Doxology, (*ad lib.*)

Praise to Thy e - ter - nal me - rit, Fa -ther, Son, and Ho - ly Spi - rit. A - men.

[26]

No. 23.   **Peniel.** (L.M.)

W. H. H., 1867.

Sun of my soul, Thou Sa - viour dear, It is not night if Thou be near;

Oh ! may no earth-born cloud a - rise To hide Thee from Thy servant's eyes. Amen.

No. 24.   **Melcombe.** (L.M)

OLD CHURCH PSALMODY.

*

Where high the heav'n-ly tem - ple stands, The house of God not made with hands,

A great High Priest our na-ture wears, The Guar-dian of man-kind ap - pears.

* Modern progression.

[27]

No. 25. **Galilee.** (L.M.)

W. H. H., 1867.

* Just as I am—with-out one plea, But that Thy blood was shed for me,

And that Thou bidd'st me come to Thee— O Lamb of God, I come, I come. A-men.

No. 26. **Cyprus.** (L.M.)

W. H. H., 1861.

Je - sus, Thou joy of lov - ing hearts, Thou Fount of Life, Thou Light of men,

From the best bliss that earth im - parts, We turn un - fill'd to Thee a - gain. A-men.

See BETHABARA, No. 222.

[28]

No. 27. **Hermon.** (L.M.)

W. H. II., 184..

When I sur - vey the wond'rous Cross On which the Prince of Glo - ry died,

My rich-est gain I count but loss, And pour con-tempt on all my pride. A-men.

No. 28. **Gethsemane.** (L.M.)

W. H. H., 1838.

Je - sus, Thy blood and right-eous - ness My beau - ty are, my glo-rious dress;

'Midst flaming worlds, in these ar - ray'd, With joy shall I lift up my head. Amen.

No. 29.   **Spires.** (L.M.)   [29]

(*See Preface, p.* xviii.)

OLD CHURCH PSALMODY.

E - ter - ni - ty! E - ter - ni - ty! That boundless, soundless, tide-less   sea,

Of mys - te - ries the mys - te - ry; What is E - ter - ni - ty to   me?

No. 30.   **Hareth.** (*Forest of*)   (L.M.)

W. H. H.

The Lord shall come! the earth shall quake, The moun-tains   to their cen - tre shake;

And, withering from the vault of   night, The stars shall pale their fee - ble   light. . . .

* Wrongly called WARTBURG.   D

No. 31.   **Hiddekel.**   (L.M.)   [30]

W. H. H.

God of my life, to Thee I call; Af-flict-ed at Thy feet I fall;

When the great water-floods pre-vail, Leave not my trembling heart to fail. A - - men.

No. 32.   **Saxony.**   (L.M.)

(See Preface, p. xviii.)

OLD CHURCH PSALMODY.

That day of wrath ! that dreadful day, When heaven and earth shall pass a - way,

What power shall be the sin - ner's stay ? How shall he meet that dread - ful day ? A-men.

No. 33.   **Rostoc.** (L.M.D.)   [31]

OLD CHURCH PSALMODY.

Be - fore th' Al-migh-ty pow'r be - gan   To form the wond'rous frame of   man ;

Be - fore He hung the lights on   high,   And made them spar-kle o'er the   sky;

Be - fore He   gave the moun-tains birth,   Or shap'd the   yet un-found-ed   earth,

God all His   ran-som'd peo - ple knew,   And   in   His   love He chose them   too.

No. 34.   𝕰𝖑𝖆𝖍. (*Valley of*)   (C.M.)   [32]

W. H. H., 1845.

All bail the pow'r of Je-su's Name, Let an-gels pros-trate fall; Bring forth the

roy-al di - a - dem, And crown Him, crown Him, crown Him "Lord of all." A-men.

No. 35.   𝕮𝖍𝖊𝖘𝖆𝖑𝖔𝖓. (*Mount*)   (C.M.)

W. H. H., 1854.

Ho - san-na! raise the peal-ing hymn To Da-vid's Son and Lord;

With Che - ru - bim and Se - ra - phim Ex - alt th'in-car-nate Word. A-men.

No. 36.   **Bether.** (*Mountains of*)   (C.M.)   [33]

W. H. H., c. 135

Sal - va - tion! O the joy - ful sound, 'Tis plea - sure to our ears!

A sove - reign balm for ev' - ry wound, A cor - dial for our fears.

Doxology.

Glo - ry, ho-nour, praise, and pow - er, Be un - to the Lamb for e - ver!

Je - sus Christ is our Re - deem - er: Hal - le - lu- jah, praise the Lord. A-men.

No. 37.　　　**Iona.** (C.M.)　　　[34]

In Scotch Scale.

W. H. H., 1869.

Isles of the deep, re-joice, re-joice! Ye ran-som'd na-tions sing

The prais-es of your Lord and God, The tri-umphs of your King. A-men.

No. 38.　　　**Eden.** (C.M.)

W. H. H., 1845.

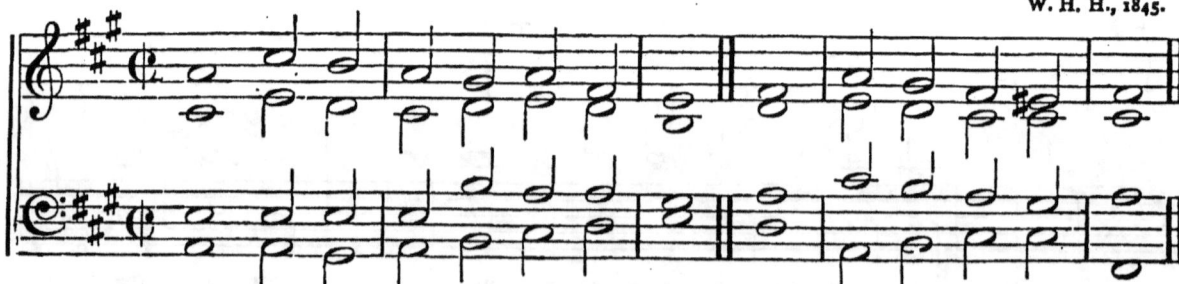

Come, let us join our cheer-ful songs With an-gels round the throne;

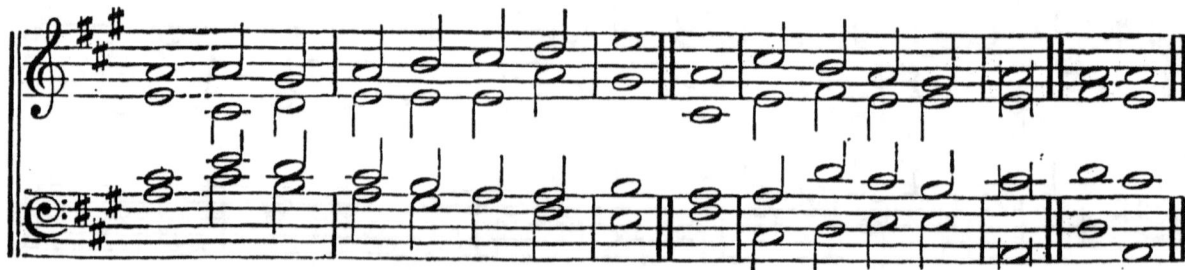

Ten thou-sand thou-sand are their tongues, But all their joys are one. A-men.

No. 39.   **Nottingham;** or, St. Magnus.   (C.M.)   [35]

OLD CHURCH PSALMODY.

The Head that once was crown'd with thorns, Is crown'd with glo - ry now ;

A roy - al di - a - dem a - dorns The migh - ty Vic - tor's brow.

No. 40.   **Gloucester.**   (C.M.)

OLD CHURCH PSALMODY.

Be - gin, my tongue, some heav'n - ly theme, And speak some boundless thing;

The migh - ty works, or migh-tier name, Of our e - ter - nal King. A - men.

No. 41   **Berachah.** (*Valley of*)   (C.M.)   [36]

W. H. H., c. 1858.

The Son of God goes forth to war, A king-ly crown to gain:

His blood-red ban-ner streams a-far; Who fol-lows in His train? A-men

No. 42.   **Kedar.**   (C.M.)

W. H. H., 1859.

My God, the cov'-nant of Thy love, A-bides for e-ver sure;

And in its match-less grace I feel My hap-pi-ness se-cure.

No. 43.　　**Bristol.** (C.M.)　　[37]

(*See Preface, p.* iv.)

OLD CHURCH PSALMODY.

Hark! the glad sound, the Sa - viour comes, The Sa - viour pro - mis'd long!

Let ev' - ry heart pre - pare a throne, And ev' - ry voice a song. A - men.

No. 44.　　**Tallis's Ordinal.** (C.M.)

(*See Preface, p.* xviii.)

OLD CHURCH PSALMODY.

Come, Ho - ly Spi - rit, heav'n - ly Dove, With all Thy quick'ning powers.;

Kin - dle a flame of sa - cred love In these cold hearts of ours. A - men.

No. 45.   **York.** (C.M.)   [38]
(*See Preface, p.* xviii.)   OLD CHURCH PSALMODY.

Be-hold! the moun-tain of the Lord   In lat-ter days shall rise

On moun-tain-tops, a-bove the hills, And draw the won-d'ring eyes. A-men.

No. 46.   **Winchester.*** (C.M.)
(*See Preface, p.* xviii.)   OLD CHURCH PSALMODY.

Give me the wings of faith to   rise   Within   the   veil, and   see

The saints a-bove, how great their joys, How   bright their glories   be.

* Wrongly called WINCHESTER OLD.

[39]

No. 47.   Nayland; OR, St. Stephen.   (C.M.)

Harmonized by W. H. H.

Je - ru - sa - lem, my hap - py home, Name e - ver dear to me.

When shall my la-bours have an end, In joy, and peace, and thee? A - men.

No. 48.   Adria.   (C.M.)

W. H. H. 1869.

As pants the hart for cool - ing streams, When heat - ed in the chase,

So pants my soul, O God, for Thee, And Thy re-fresh-ing grace. A - men.

[40]

No. 49.   **St. James.** (C.M.)

OLD CHURCH PSALMODY.

Thou art the Way: to Thee a - lone   From sin and death we   flee,

And   he who would the Fa - ther seek,   Must seek Him, Lord, by   Thee.   A - men.

No. 50.   **Melross.** (C.M.)

OLD CHURCH PSALMODY.

Fa - ther of mer - cies,   in Thy word What end - less glo - ry shines!

For e - ver be Thy name a-dor'd, For these ce - les - tial   lines.   A - men.

No. 51.   **Besor.** (*Brook*) (C.M.)

[4]

W. H. H., 1835.

What shall I ren-der to my God For all His kind-ness shown?

My feet shall vi-sit Thine a-bode, My songs ad-dress Thy throne. A-men.

No. 52.   **St. Ann.** (C.M.)

(*See Preface, p.* xviii.)

OLD CHURCH PSALMODY.

Now, gra-cious Lord, Thine arm re-veal, And make Thy glo-ry known;

Now let us all Thy pre-sence feel, And soft-en hearts of stone. A-men.

No. 53.   **St. Chrysostom.**   (C.M.)   [42]
(*See Preface, p. xix.*)

W. H. H., circ. 1830.

Wake, harp of Zi - on, wake a - gain, Up - on thine an - cient hill,

On Jor-dan's long - de - sert - ed plain, By Ke-dron's low - ly rill.   A - men.

No. 54.   **Evan I.**   (C.M.)
(*See Preface, p. xix.*)

W. H. H., Melody, July, 1846.
Harmony, March 19, 1870.

Je - sus, the ve - ry thought of Thee With sweet-ness fills my breast;

But sweet - er far Thy face to see, And in Thy pre-sence rest. A-men.

No. 55.   **London New;** OR, NEWTON. (C.M.)   [43]
(*See Preface, p. xix.*)

OLD CHURCH PSALMODY.

O God, our help in a - ges past, Our hope for years to come,

Our shel - ter from the storm - y blast, And our e - ter - nal home. A - men.

No. 56.   **Caithness.** (C.M.)

OLD CHURCH PSALMODY.

Plung'd in a gulf of dark de - spair We wretch - ed sin - ners lay,

With - out one cheer - ful beam of hope, Or spark of glim' - ring day.

No. 57.   **Ephron.** (*Mount*)   (C.M.)   [44]

W. H. H., 1838.

When all Thy mer-cies, O my God, My ris-ing soul sur-veys;

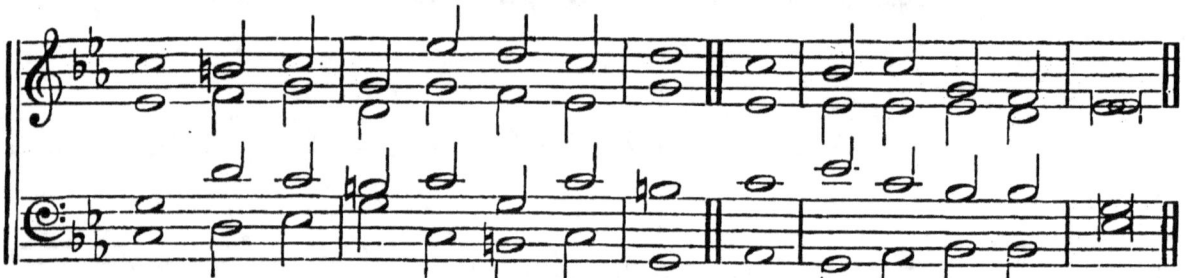

Trans-port-ed with the view, I'm lost In won-der, love, and praise.

No. 58.   **St. Matthias.**

(*See Preface, p. xix.*)

OLD CHURCH PSALMODY.

Our God is love; and all His saints His m-age bear be-low:

The heart with love to God in-spir'd, With love to man will glow. A-men.

No. 59.   **Arran.** (C.M.)   [45]

In Scotch Scale.   W. H. H., 1869.

Oh, what a lone - ly path were ours, Could we, O Fa - ther, see

No home of rest be - yond it all, No guide or help in Thee!

No. 60.   **St. David.** (C.M.)

(See Preface, p. xix.)

OLD CHURCH PSALMODY.

God moves in a mys - te - rious way, His won-ders to per - form;

He plants His foot-steps in the sea, And rides up - on the storm.

c

No. 61. **Carlisle.** (C.M.) [46]

OLD CHURCH PSALMODY.

For mer-cies, countless as the sands, Which dai-ly I re-ceive

From Je-sus, my Re-deem-er's hands, My soul, what canst thou give?

No 62. **Salisbury.** (C.M.)

OLD CHURCH PSALMODY.

In-car-nate God! The soul that knows Thy name's mys-te-rious power,

Shall dwell in un-dis-turb'd re-pose, Nor fear the try-ing hour.

No. 63..   **Kent.** (C.M.)   [47]

OLD CHURCH PSALMODY.

When I can read my ti - tle clear To man-sions in the skies,

I bid fare - well to ev - 'ry fear, And wipe my weeping eyes. A - men.

No. 64.   **Dimon.** (*Waters of*) (C.M.)

Composed in a dream.

W. H. H., 1855.

Why should the chil-dren of a King, Go mourn-ing all their days?

Great Com-fort-er, des-cend, and bring Some to-kens of Thy grace. A - men.

[48]

No. 65. **French**; OR, DUNDEE. (C.M.)

OLD CHURCH PSALMODY.

How sweet the name of Je - sus sounds, In a be - liev - er's ear,

It soothes his sor-rows, heals his wounds, And drives a - way his fear. A - men.

No. 66. **Bedford.** (C.M.)

(*See Preface p. xx.*)

OLD CHURCH PSALMODY.

Through all the changing scenes of life, In trou - ble and in joy,

The prais - es of my God shall still My heart and tongue em - ploy.

No. 66 *a.*   **Bedford.** (C.M.)   (Common Time.)   [49]

Harmonized by W. H. H.

Oh! for a heart to praise my God, A heart from sin set free;

A heart that al - ways feels Thy blood, So free - ly shed for me. A - men.

No. 67.   **Farrant.** (C.M.)

(*See Preface, p.* xx.)

OLD CHURCH PSALMODY.

The saints on earth, and those a - bove, But one com - mu - nion make,

Join'd to their Lord in bonds of love. All of His grace par - take. A - men

No. 68.   **Dunfermline.*** (C.M.)   [50]

OLD CHURCH PSALMODY.

O Thou, from whom all good-ness flows, I lift my heart to Thee;

In all my sor-rows, con-flicts, woes, Good Lord! re-mem-ber me. A-men.

No. 69.   **Carmel.** (*Mount*) (C.M.)

W. H. H.

Lord, as to Thy dear cross we flee, And plead to be for-giv'n,

So let Thy life our pat-tern be, And form our souls for heav'n. A-men.

* Wrongly called SOUTHAM.

No. 70.   **Chester.**   [51]
Or, "A Prayer for the Queen's Most Excellent Majestie."
(See Preface, p. xx.)

OLD CHURCH PSALMODY.

Lord, when we bend be-fore Thy throne, And our con-fes-sions pour,

Teach us to feel the sins we own, And hate what we de-plore. A-men.

No. 71.   **Culross.**   (C.M.)

OLD CHURCH PSALMODY.

A pil-grim through this lone-ly world, The bless-ed Sa-viour pass'd;

A mourn-er all His life was He, A dy-ing Lamb at last.

No. 72.   **Dundee; or, Windsor.** (C.M.)   [52]
                    (See Preface, p. xx.)
                                                                    OLD CHURCH PSALMODY.

O help us, Lord! each hour of need   Thy heav'n-ly suc-cour   give;

Help   us   in thought, and word, and deed,   Each hour on earth we   live.   A-men.

No. 73.   **St. Mary's; or, Hackney.** (C.M.)
                    (See Preface p. xx.)
                                                                    Harmonized by W. H. H.

Al - migh - ty   God, be - fore Thy throne   Thy mourn-ing peo - ple   bend;

'Tis on Thy sov'reign grace a - lone   Our hum-ble hopes de - pend.   A - men.

No. 74.   **Old Xlibth.** (C.M.D.,   [53]

OLD CHURCH PSALMODY.

He came, whose em - bas - sy was peace; He left His throne a - bove

To prove if en - mi - ty would cease Be - neath the pow'r of love.

He came, whose er - rand was to give, His hand was o - pen'd wide;

Yea, at our need, that we might live, He gave Him - self, and died.

No. 75.   **Old Lxxxi^st.** (C.M.D.   [54]

(*See Preface, p. xx.*)

OLD CHURCH PSALMODY.

Je - ru - sa - lem! Je - ru - sa lem! En-thron-ed once on high,

Thou fa-vour'd home of God on earth, Thou heav'n be - low the sky;

Now brought to bond - age with thy sons, A curse and grief to see;

Je - ru - sa - lem! Je - ru - sa - lem! Our tears shall flow for thee.

No. 76.   **Bethaven.** (*Wilderness of*) (C.M.D) [55]

W. H. H.

The ros - eate hues of ear - ly dawn, The bright-ness of the day,

The crim - son of the sun - set sky, How fast they fade a - way!

Oh, for the pear - ly gates of heav'n! Oh, for the gold - en floor!

Oh, for the Sun of Right-eous - ness, That set - teth ne - ver more! A - men.

No. 77.   **Evan II.** (C.M.D.)   [56]
(See Preface, p. xix.)

W. H. H. 1846.

I heard the voice of Je - sus say, "Come un - to me and rest;

Lay down, thou wea - ry one, lay down Thy head up - on my breast."

I came to Je - sus as I was, Wea - ry, and worn, and sad;

I found in Him a rest - ing-place, And He has made me glad. A - men.

No. 78.   **Old Nunc Dimittis.** (C.M.D)   [57]

OLD CHURCH PSALMODY.

See what un-bound-ed zeal and love In - flam'd the Sa-viour's breast,

When sted - fast tow'rds Je - ru - sa - lem His ur - gent way He prest.

Good will to man, and zeal for God, His ev -'ry thought en - gross;

He longs to be bap - tiz'd with blood, He thirsts to reach the Cross.

* Raised from the Dominant to the Tonic.

No. 79. **Aven.** (*PLAIN OF*) (S.M.) [58]

W. H. H. 1841.

A - wake, and sing the song Of Mo - ses and the Lamb;

Wake, ev - 'ry heart and ev - 'ry tongue, To praise the Sa-viour's name. A - men.

No. 80. **Narenza.** (S.M.)

OLD CHURCH PSALMODY.

Stand up, and bless the Lord, Ye peo - ple of his choice;

Stand up, and bless the Lord your God, With heart, and soul, and voice. A - men.

No 81.   **Abana.** (*River*) (S.M.)   [59]

W. H. H.

Come, ye that love the Lord, And let your joys be known;

Join in a song with sweet ac - cord, And thus sur-round the throne. A - men.

No. 82.   **Swabia.** (S.M.)

OLD CHURCH PSALMODY.

To God, the on - ly wise, Our Sa - viour and our King,

Let all the saints be - low the skies Their hum - ble prais - es bring. A - men.

No. 83.   𝔐𝔬𝔯𝔞𝔳𝔦𝔞.* (s.m.)   [60]

OLD CHURCH PSALMODY.

Ye ser-vants of the Lord, Each in his of-fice wait,

Ob - serv-ant of His heav'n - ly word, And watch-ful at His gate.

No. 84.   𝔄𝔪𝔞𝔫𝔞. (*MOUNT*)   (s.m.)

W. H. H., 1838.

Come to Thy tem - ple, Lord, Thy wait - ing church to bless:

Let here Thy glo - ry be a - dor'd, Give here Thy word suc - cess.   A - men.

* Wrongly called TYTHERTON, or PRAGUE.

No. 85. **St. Michael.** (S.M.) [61]

(*See Preface, p. xxi.*)

OLD CHURCH PSALMODY.

To bless Thy cho-sen race, In mer-cy, Lord, in-cline;

And cause the bright-ness of Thy face On all Thy saints to shine. A-men.

No. 86. **Ajalon.** (*VALLEY OF*) (S.M.)

W. H. H.

. Not all the blood of beasts On Jew-ish al-tars slain,

Could give the guilt-y con-science peace, Or wash a-way the stain.

No. 87.   **Franconia.** (s.m.)   [62]

OLD CHURCH PSALMODY.

Be - hold the throne of grace! The pro - mise calls me near;

There Je - sus shows a smil - ing face, And waits to an - swer prayer. A - men.

No. 88.   **Achor.** (*VALLEY OF*) (s.m.)

W. H. H., 1847.

I was a wan-d'ring sheep, I did not love the fold;

I did not love my Shep-herd's voice, I would not be con - troll'd.

No. 89.   **Abarim.** (*MOUNT*)   (S.M.)   [63]

W. H. H.

Sow   in   the morn   thy   seed;   At   eve   hold   not   thy   hand;

To   doubt   and   fear   give   thou   no   heed,   Broad - cast   it   o'er   the   land.

No. 90.   **Armageddon.** (*VALLEY OF*)   (S.M.)

W. H. H., 1841.

Come,   Ho - ly   Spi - rit,   come!   Let   Thy   bright beams   a - - rise;

Dis - pel   all   sor - row from   our minds,   All   dark-ness from   our   eyes.   A - men.

No. 91.   **Jeruel**; (*Wilderness of*) or, **Hawkstone**.   (S.M.)   [64]

W. H. H., 1869.

What cheer - ing words are these! Their sweet - ness who can tell!

In time, and to e - ter - nal days, 'Tis with the righ - teous well.

No. 92.   **Cyrene**.   (S.M.)

W. H. H., 1860.

Be - hold, what won - drous grace The Fa - ther hath be - stowed

On sin - ners of a mor - tal race, To call them sons of God! A - men.

No. 93.   **Marano.** (s.m.)   [65]

(See Preface p. xxi.)

OLD CHURCH PSALMODY.

And will the Judge de - scend, And must the dead a - rise,

And not a sin - gle soul es - cape, His all - dis - cern - ing eyes?

No. 94.   **Southwell.** (s.m.)

(See Preface, p. xxi.)

OLD CHURCH PSALMODY.

In sor - row and dis - tress, To Thee, O Lord, we fly;

In pe - ni - ten - tial low - li - ness, To Thee for mer - cy cry. A - men.

No. 95.   **Ludlow.** (s.m.)   [66]
                                                          OLD CHURCH PSALMODY.

Far   from my heav'n-ly   home,   Far   from my   Fa-ther's breast,

Faint-ing I cry, blest Spi-rit, come, And speed me to   my rest. A - men.

No. 95a.   **St. Bride.** (s.m.)
                                                          OLD CHURCH PSALMODY

Have mer-cy, Lord, on   me,   As   Thou wert ev - er   kind;

Let me, op-prest with loads of guilt, Thy wont-ed mer-cy find. A - men.

No. 96.   **Massah.** (*THE ROCK*)   (S.M.D.)   [67]

W. H. H.

Thou art gone up - on high, To man - sions in the sky!

And round Thy throne un - ceas - ing - ly The songs of praise a - rise.

But we are linger - ing here, With sin and care op - press'd;

Lord, send Thy pro - mis'd Com - fort - er, And lead us to our rest! A - men.

No. 97.   𝕺𝖑𝖉 𝕴𝖗𝖛ᵗᵇ· (S.M.D.)   [68]

OLD CHURCH PSALMODY.

The Church has wait - ed long Her ab - sent Lord to see;

And still in lone - li - ness she waits, A friend - less strang - er she.

Age af - ter age has gone, Sun af - ter sun has set,

And still in weeds of wid - ow - hood, She weeps, a mourn - er yet.
Come then, Lord Je - su, come! A - men.

No. 98.   St. Silas.*   55,55, 65, 65.

[69]

F. R. H., 1870.

Breast the wave, Chris - tian, When it is strong - est;

Watch for day, Chris - tian, When the night's long - est;

On - ward and up - ward still, Be thine en - dea - vour;

The rest that re - main - eth Will be for e - ver.

* This Tune may be sung in Triple Time, if a more subdued effect is desired.

No. 99.　　　　**Zophim.** (*Field of*)　55, 7777, 6.　　[70]

W. H. H.

There was joy in heav'n! There was joy in heav'n!

When this good - ly world to frame, The Lord of might and

mer - cy came; Shouts of joy were heard on high,

And the stars sang from the sky, "Glo - ry to God in heav'n." A - men.

No. 100.   𝕹𝖎𝖒𝖗𝖎𝖒. (VALLEY OF)   64, 64, 664.   [71]

W. H. H., 1857.

Near - er, my God, to Thee, Near - er to Thee!

E'en though it be a cross That rais - eth me,

Still all my song shall be— Near - er, my

God, to Thee, Near - er to Thee! A - men.

No. 101.   **Olivet.*** (*Mount*)   64,64,664.   [72]

W. H. H., 1857.

Near - er, my God, to Thee, Near - er to Thee! E'en though it

be a cross That rai - seth me; Still all my song shall be—

Near - er, my God, to Thee, Near - er to Thee! A - men.

No. 102.   **Beulah.**   64,64,6664.

W. H. H., 1866.

I'm but a stran-ger here, Heav'n is my home; Earth is a de - sert drear,

* Or, Ophel.

[73]

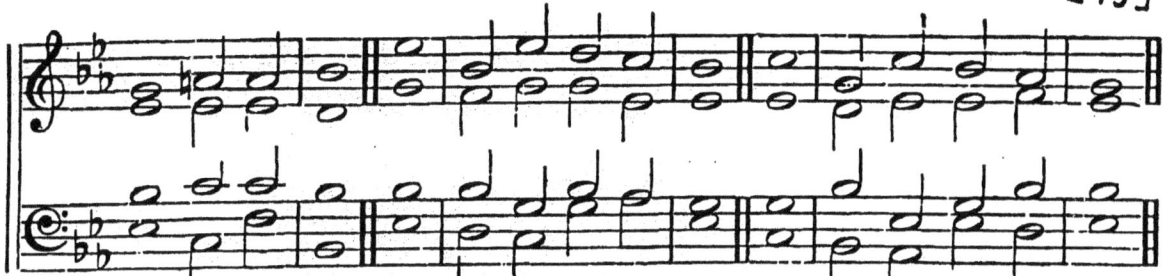

Heav'n is my home; Dan-ger and sor-row stand Round me on ev'-ry hand;

Heav'n is my fa-ther-land, Heav'n is my home.

No. 103. **Amplias.** 64,66.

F. R. H., 1870.

The sun is sink-ing fast, The day-light dies;

Let love a-wake and pay Her ev'n-ing sa-cri-fice. A-men.

[74]

No. 104.   **Claudia.**   65,65.

F. R. H., 1870.

Je - su, meek and gen - tle, Son of God most High,

Pity - ing, lov - ing Sa - viour, Hear Thy chil - dren's cry. A - men.

No. 105.   **Hermas.**   65, 65 D, OR 65, 12 LINES.

F. R. H., 1870.

Earth be - low is teem - ing, Heav'n is bright a - bove,

Ev' - ry brow is beam - ing In the light of love.

[75]

Ev'-ry eye re-joi-ces, Ev'-ry thought is praise;

Hap-py hearts and voi-ces Glad-den nights and days.

CHORUS.

O Al-migh-ty Giv-er, Boun-ti-ful and free,

As the joy in har-vest, Joy we be-fore Thee. A-men.

No. 106   **St. Barnabas.**   65,65. D.   [76]

F. R. H., 1870.

In the hour of tri - al, Je - su, pray for me,

Lest, by base de - ni - al, I de - part from Thee.

When Thou see'st me wa - ver, With a look re - call,

Nor, for fear or fa - vour, Suf - fer me to fall. A - men.

No. 107.   **Moscow.*** 664,6664..

[77]

OLD CHURCH PSALMODY.

Sound, sound the truth a - broad, Bear ye the

word of God Through the wide world;

Tell what our Lord has done; Tell how the day is won,

And from his lof - ty throne Sa - tan is hurl'd. A - men.

* Wrongly called TRINITY, or BENTICK.

E

No. 108.   **Oreb.** (*Rock of*)   664,6664.   [78]

W. H. H.

Glo - ry to God on high! Let heav'n and

earth re - ply, Praise ye His name! His love and

grace a - dore, Who all our sor - rows bore; Sing a - loud

ev - er - more, "Wor - - thy the Lamb!" A - - men.

No. 109. **Ono.** (*Plains of*) 664,6664. [79]

W. H. H., cir. 1825.

Thou, whose Al - migh - ty word, Cha - os and

Dark - ness heard, And took their flight. Hear us, we

hum - bly pray, And where Thy gos - pel day Sheds not its

glo - rious ray, "Let there be light!" A - men.

No. 110.   𝕾𝖙𝖔𝖇𝖊𝖑.   664,6664.   [80]
                                                        OLD CHURCH PSALMODY.

My   faith   looks   up   to   Thee,   Thou

Lamb   of   Cal - va - ry,   Sa - viour   di - vine!   Now

hear   me   while   I   pray: Take   all   my   guilt a - way;   O

let   me   from   this   day   Be   whol - ly   Thine.   A - men.

No. 111.   **Damaris.**   66,66.   [81]

F. R. H., 1870.

Lord, Thy word a - bid - eth, And our foot - steps guid - eth;

Who its truth be - liev - eth, Light and joy re - ceiv - eth. A - men.

No. 112.   **Bashan.** (*HILL OF*)   66,66.

W. H. H.

Thy way, not mine, O Lord, How - ev - er dark it be;

Lead me by Thine own hand; Choose out the path for me.

No. 113.   **Psalm cxlviii.***   6666, 4444.   [82]

(New Version.)

OLD CHURCH PSALMODY.

Christ is our cor-ner stone, On Him a-

-lone we build; With His true saints a-lone The

courts of heav'n are fill'd: On His great love Our

hopes we place Of pre-sent grace, And joys a-bove.

* Wrongly called ALNWICK.

No. 114.   **Psalm cxlviii**.* 6666, 4444.   [83]
(Old Version.)

OLD CHURCH PSALMODY.

Lord   of   the   worlds   a - - bove,   How   plea - sant

and   how   fair,   The   dwell - ings   of   Thy   love,   Thy

earth - ly . tem - ples   are !   To   Thine   a - bode   My

heart   as - pires,   With   warm   de - sires,   To   see   my   God.

* Wrongly called BODMIN.

No. 115.   𝕲𝖔𝖕𝖘𝖆𝖑.*   6666, 4444.   [84]

OLD CHURCH PSALMODY

Blow ye the trum - pet, blow,.......... The glad - ly so - lemn

sound; Let all the na - tions know,........... To

earth's re - mot - est bound, The year of Ju - bi -

- lee is come, Re - turn, ye ran - som'd sin - ners, home.

* Wrongly called KNARESBOROUGH.

No. 116.   **Baca.** (*VALLEY OF*)   6666, 66.   [85]

W. H. H., 1852.

I gave my life for thee, My pre - cious blood I shed

That thou might'st ran - som'd be, And quick - en'd from the dead.

I gave my life for thee: What hast thou giv'n for Me?

No. 117.　　　　　𝔖𝔥𝔢𝔟𝔞.　6666 D.*　　　　　[86]

W. H. H., 1865.

There　is　a　bless : ed　home　Be - yond　this　land　of　woe,

Where　tri - als　nev - er　come,　Nor　tears　of　sor - row　flow;

Where　faith　is　lost　in　sight,　And　pa - tient　hope　is　crown'd,

* For 666,666 omit 3rd and 4th strains.　For 66, 66, 66 omit 5th and 6th strains.
For 86,86,6666 repeat the last note of 1st and 3rd strains, thus—

[87]

And ev - er - last - ing light Its glo - ry throws a - round. A - men.

No. 118.   **Arnon.** (*The river*)   66, 84.

W. H. H., 1841.

Be - hold the Lamb of God! Be - hold, be - lieve, and live :

Be - hold His all - a - ton - ing blood, And life re - ceive.

No. 119.　　　**Moriah.** (*Mount*)　6666, 88.　　[88]

W. H. H., 1846.

Re - joice, the Lord is King, Your

Lord and King a - dore; Mor - tals, give thanks and sing, And

tri - umph ev - er - more: Lift up your hearts, lift up your voice; Re -

- joice a - gain I say, ... re - joice. A - men.

No. 120.   **Mizpeh.** (*VALLEY OF*)   6666, 88.   [89]

W. H. H., 1851.

We   give   im - mor - tal   praise   To

God   the   Fa - ther's   love,   For   all   our   com - forts   here,   And

bet - ter   hopes   a - bove;   He   sent   His   own   e -

- ter - nal   Son   To   die   for   sins   that   man   had   done.   A - men.

No. 121. **Nebo.** (*Mount*) 6666, 88. [90]

W. H. H., 1848.

Join all the glo - rious names Of wis - dom, love, and power, That

ev - er mor - tals knew, That an - gels ev - er bore: All are too mean to

speak His worth, Too mean to set my Sa - - viour forth.

No. 122. **Megiddon.** (*Valley of*) 66, 86, 88.

W. H. H.

I need no o - ther plea With which t' ap-proach my God,

[91]

Than His own mer-cy, bound-less, free, Through Christ on man be-stow'd:

A Father's love, a Father's care Re-ceives and answers ev'-ry prayer.

No. 123.   **Trophimus.**   669.

F. R. H., 1870.

Spared a lit-tle long-er, May our souls grow strong-er,

To main-tain the ar-duous fight of faith. A-men.

No. 124. **Enon.** 67, 87.

[92]

F. R. H., 1870.

Thou great mys - te - rious Lord! We sin - ners now ad - dress Thee,

In ho - ly fear would we draw near, With rev'rence now to bless Thee. A - - - men.

No. 125. **Goshen.** 76, 76.*

W. H. H., 1863.

O faint and fee - ble - heart - ed! Why thus cast down with fear?

Fresh aid shall be im - part - ed, Thy God, un - seen, is near. A - men.

* For the same measure, see No. 130.

No. 126.   𝔐inden.   76, 76, 77.   [93]

OLD CHURCH PSALMODY.

Je - sus,   Sun   and   Shield   art   Thou,   Sun   and

Shield   for   e - - ver!   Ne - ver   canst   Thou   cease   to

shine,   Cease   to   guard   us   ne - - ver.   Cheer   our

steps   as   on   we   go,   Come   be - tween   us   and   the   foe.

F

No. 127.   **Zoan E.** (*Field of*)   76, 76 D.   [94]

W. H. H., 1845.

From Green-land's i - cy moun-tains, From In - dia's co - ral strand,

Where Af - ric's sun - ny foun - - tains Roll down their gold - en sand;

From many an an - cient ri - ver, From many a palm - y plain,

They call us to de - li - ver Their land from er - ror's chain! A - men.

No. 128.

Zeboim. (*Valley of*) 76, 76 D.

[95]

W. H. II., cir. 1858.

Some - times a light sur - pri - ses The Chris - tian while he sings;

It is the Lord who ri - ses, With heal - ing in His wings;

When com - forts are de - clin - ing, He grants the soul a - gain

A sea - son of clear shin - ing, To cheer it af - ter rain.

No. 129. **Mahanaim.** 76, 76. D. [96]

W. H. H., Jan. 1870.

I lay my sins on Je - sus, The spot - less Lamb of God;

He bears them all, and frees us From the ac - curs - ed load.

I bring my guilt to Je - sus, To wash my crim - son stains,

White in His blood most pre - cious, Till not a spot re - mains.

No. 130. (PART I.)   **Goldbach.** *   76, 76. D.

[97]

OLD CHURCH PSALMODY.

O Day of rest and glad - ness, O Day of joy and light;

O balm of care and sad - ness, Most beau - ti - ful, most bright;

(PART II.)

On thee the high and low - ly, Through a - ges joined in tune,

Sing ho - ly, ho - ly, ho - ly, To the great God Tri - une. A - men.

* Either half of this tune may be used for 76, 76, single. Part I. is known as HEIDELBERG, or LINCOLN.

No. 131.   **Gareb.** (HILL OF) 76, 76, 77, 76.   [98]

W. H. H., 1841.

Rise, my soul, and stretch thy wings, Thy bet - ter por - tion trace;

Rise from tran - si - to - ry things, Tow'rds heav'n, thy na - tive place:

Sun, and moon, and stars de - cay, Time shall soon this earth re - move;

Rise, my soul, and haste a - way, To seats pre-par'd a - bove. A - men.

No. 132.   **Kiriathaim.** (*Valley of*)   76, 86, 86, 86.   [99]

W. H. H., 1869.

We won't give up the Bi - ble, God's ho - ly Book of truth;

The bless - ed staff of hoar - y age, The guide of ear - ly youth;

The lamp that sheds a glo - rious light On, else, a drear - y road;

The voice that speaks a Sa - viour's love, And leads us home to God.

No. 131. **Gareb.** (*HILL OF*) 76, 76, 77, 76. [180]

W. H. H., 1841.

Rise, my soul, and stretch thy wings, Thy bet - ter por - tion trace;

Rise from tran - si - to - ry things, Tow'rds heav'n, thy na - tive place:

Sun, and moon, and stars de - cay, Time shall soon this earth re - move;

Rise, my soul, and haste a - way, To seats pre - par'd a - bove. A - men.

No. 132.   **Kiriathaim.** (*Valley of*)   76, 86, 86, 86.   [101]

W. H. H., 1869.

We won't give up the Bi - ble, God's ho - ly Book of truth;

The bless - ed staff of hoar - y age, The guide of ear - ly youth;

The lamp that sheds a glo - rious light On, else, a drear - y road;

The voice that speaks a Sa - viour's love, And leads us home to God.

No. 133.   **Havergal.** 777, or 777 D.   [102]

This was the last music by W.H.H.,   (*See No.* 163.)

composed the day before his death.   W. H. H., April 16, 1870.

Je - sus,   to Thy ta - ble led,   Now let ev - 'ry heart be fed,

With   the   true   and liv - ing bread.   A - - - - - men.

No. 134.   **Ramah.** 777.

                                                            W. H. H., 1861.

Ho - ly   Ghost,   my   Com - fort - er !   Now   from

high - est heav'n ap - pear, Shed Thy gra - cious ra - diance here.   A - men.

[103]

No. 135.　　　**Samos.**　777, 3.

W. H. H., 1859.

"Chris - tian! seek not yet re - pose;" Hear thy

guar-dian an - gel say; Thou art in the midst of foes. "Watch and pray!"

No. 136.　　　**Shenir E.** (*Mount*)　777, 5.

W. H. H., 1850.

Lord of mer - cy, and of might, Ma - ker, Teach - er, In - fi - nite,

rall.

Of man - kind the life and light, Je - sus, hear and save A - men.

No. 137.   **Pisgah.** (*Mount*)   77, 77.

W. H. H., 1838.

[104]

Hark! the song of ju - bi - lee, Loud as

migh - ty thun - ders roar, Or the ful - ness

of the sea, When it breaks up - on the shore.

Hal - le - lu - jah, Hal - le - lu - jah! A - men.

No. 138.   **Abilene.**   77,77.   [105]

W. H. H., 1866.

Christ the Lord is ris'n to - day, Sons of

men, and an - gels, say! Raise your songs and

tri - umphs high: Sing, ye heav'ns; thou earth re - ply!

Hal - le - lu - jah, Hal - le - lu - jah! A - men

No. 139.   **Lubeck.**   77, 77.   [106]

OLD CHURCH PSALMODY.

Let us with a glad - some mind, Praise the

Lord, for He is kind; For His mer - cies

shall en - dure, Ev - er faith - ful, ev - er sure.

Hal - le - lu - jah, Hal - le - lu - jah! A - men.

No. 140.

Judea. 77, 77.

[107]

W. H. H., 1854.

Je - sus Christ is ris'n to - day, Hal - le - lu - jah!

Our tri - um - phant ho - ly day, Hal - le - lu - jah!

Who did once up - on the cross, (Hal - le - lu - jah!) Suf - fer

to re - deem our loss, Hal - le - lu - jah, Hal - le - lu - jah! A - men.

No. 141.   **Rephaim.** (*Valley of*) 77, 77.

W. H. H.

Christ the Lord is ris'n a - gain. Christ hath bro - ken ev - 'ry chain;

Hark, an - ge - lic voi - ces cry, Sing - ing ev - er - more on high,

Al - - - le - lu - ia, Al - - - le - lu - ia! A - men.

No. 142.   **Sephar.** (*Mount*) 77, 77.

W. H. H., 1854.

Sirg, O heav'ns! O earth, re - joice! An - gel harp, and hu - man voice,

[109]

Round Him, as He ri - ses, raise Your as - cend - ing Sa - viour's praise.

Al - le - lu - ia, Al - le - lu - ia ! A - men.

No. 143.   Perazim. (MOUNT)   77, 77.

W. H. H.

Con-q'ring kings their ti - tles take, From the foes they cap - tive make;

Je - sus, by a no - bler deed, From the thou-sands He hath freed.

No. 144.   **Pison,** (*River of*) **77, 77.**

[110]

W. H. H.

Oft in sor-row, oft in woe. On-ward, Chris-tians, on-ward go;

Fight the fight, main-tain the strife, Strengthen'd by the bread of life.

No. 145.   **Chios.** **77, 77.**

W. H. H., 1859.

Lov-ing Shep-herd of Thy sheep, Keep me, Lord, in safe-ty keep;

No-thing can Thy power withstand; None can pluck me from Thy hand. A - men.

No. 146.　　　　**Oldenburg.**　77, 77.*

[111]

OLD CHURCH PSALMODY.

Bre - thren, let us join to bless Christ, the Lord, our Righ - teous - ness;

Let our praise to Him be giv'n, High at God's right hand in heav'n. A - men.

No. 147.　　　　**Patmos.**　77, 77.

W. H. H., 1869.

Thine for ev - er! God of love, Hear us from Thy throne a - bove;

Thine for ev - er may we be, Here and in e - ter - ni - ty. A - men.

* For 76, 76 slur the 5th and 6th notes of 2nd and 4th strains.

G

No. 148.   **Gibbons.***   77, 77.   [112]

(*See Preface, p.* xxi.)   OLD CHURCH PSALMODY.

Hap-py Chris-tian! God's own child, Cho-sen, call'd, and re-con-ciled;

Once a reb-el, far from God, Now brought nigh by Je-su's blood.

No. 149.   **Vienna.**   77, 77.   OLD CHURCH PSALMODY.

Chil-dren of the heav'n-ly King, As ye jour-ney, sweet-ly sing,

Sing your Saviour's wor-thy praise, Glo-rious in His works and ways. A-men.

* Wrongly called WHITEHALL.

No. 150.　　**Rimmon.** (*Rock of*)　77, 77.　　[113]

W. H. H.

Soft - ly　now　the　light　of　day　Fades up - on　my　sight　a - way;

Free from　care, from　la - bour　free,　Lord,　I　would commune with　Thee!　A - men.

No. 151.　　**Shenir II.** (*Mount*)　77, 77.

W. H. H., 1850.

Hark!　my　soul,　it　is　the　Lord;　'Tis　thy　Sa - viour,—hear His　word;

Je - sus　speaks, and speaks to　thee: "Say,　poor　sin - ner, lov'st thou　Me?"

No. 152. **Luxemburg.** 77, 77. [114]

OLD CHURCH PSALMODY.

Ho-ly Spir-it, from on high, Bend on us a pi-tying eye;

An-i-mate the drooping heart, Bid the pow'r of sin de-part. A-men.

No. 153. **Siloam.** (POOL OF) 77, 77.

W. H. H.

In the sun, and moon, and stars, Signs and won-ders there shall be;

Earth shall quake with in-ward wars, Na-tions with per-plex-i-ty.

No. 154.   **Marah.**   77, 77.   [115]

W. H. H., 1861.

See the des - tin'd day a - rise, See a will - ing

sa - cri - fice; Je - sus, to re - deem our loss,

Hangs up - on the shame - ful cross. A - men........

No. 155.   𝔑assau.*   77, 77, 77.

[116]

OLD CHURCH PSALMODY.

Sing, O sing, this bless - ed morn, Un - to
us a Child is born, Un - to us a Son is
giv'n, God Him - self comes down from heav'n; Sing, O
sing, this bless - ed morn, Je - sus Christ to - day is born.

* Wrongly called ROSENMÜLLER.

No. 156.   **Pharpar.** (*River*)   77, 77, 77.*   [1/7]
                                                              W. H. H.

Glo - ry,   glo - ry   to   our   King!   Crowns un - fad - ing

wreathe His   head;   Je - sus   is   the   name   we   sing;

Je - sus,   ris - en   from   the   dead;   Je - sus,   spoil - er

of   the   grave,   Je - sus,   migh - ty   now   to   save.   A - men.

* For 75, 75, 77 omit the notes in [ ].

No. 157. **Ratisbon.** 77, 77, 77. [118]

OLD CHURCH PSALMODY.

Christ, whose glo - ry fills the skies, Christ the true, the on - ly Light, Sun of Righ - teous - ness, a - rise, Tri - umph o'er the shades of night: Day - spring from on high, be near; Day - star, in my heart ap - pear. A - men.

No. 158.   **Sihor.** (*River*)   77, 77, 77.

[119]

W. H. H., 1851.

Rock of a - ges, cleft for me, Let me hide my -

self in Thee; Let the wa - ter and the blood,

From Thy riv - en side which flow'd, Be of sin the

dou - ble cure, Cleanse me from its guilt and pow'r. A - men.

No. 159.　　　　**Kadesh.**　77, 77 D, or 10 lines 7s.*　　[120]

W. H. H., 1869.

Come, O come, in pi - ous lays, Sound we God Al - migh - ty's praise;
Hi - ther bring, in one con - sent, Heart, and voice, and in - stru - ment.

Mu - sic add of ev' - ry kind, Sound the trump, the cor - net wind;

Strike the vi - ol, touch the lute; Let no tongue nor string be mute,

Nor a crea - ture dumb be found, That hath ei - ther voice or sound. A - men.

* For 10 lines 7s repeat 1st and 2nd strains.

No. 160.   **Heshbon;** OR, PARRACOMBE.   **77, 77, D.**   [121]

W. H. H., 1869.

Come, ye thank-ful peo-ple, come, Raise the song of har-vest-home;

All is safe-ly ga-ther'd in, Ere the win-ter-storms be - gin.

God, our Ma-ker, doth pro - vide For our wants to be sup · plied;

Come to God's own tem-ple, come, Raise the song of har-vest-home. A - men.

No. 161.   **Seir.** (MOUNT)   **77,77** D.   [122]

W. H. H., 1850.

Je - su, Lo - ver of my soul, Let me to Thy bo - som fly;

While the near - er wa - ters roll, While the tem - pest still is high:

Hide me, O my Sa - viour, hide, Till the storm of life be past:

Safe in - to the ha - ven guide, O re - ceive my soul at last. A - men.

No. 162.   **Samaria.** (*Hill of*)   77, 77, D.

[123]

W. H. H.

Who are these ar - rayed in white, Bright - er than the noon - day sun?

Fore - most of the sons of light, Near-est the e - ter - nal throne?

These are they that bore the cross, No - bly for their Mas - ter stood,

Suf - ferers in His righ-teous cause Followers of the Christ of God.

No. 163.

the last music by W.H.H.

Habergal. 777, 777, 777.

(*See Preface, p. xxi.*)

[124]

W. H. H., April 16, 1870.

Migh - ty Fa - ther! Bless-ed Son! Ho - ly Spi - rit! Three in One! E - ver -

- more Thy will be done! Threefold is Thy glo-rious might, Three-fold is Thy

name of light, Ho - ly! Aw - ful! In - fi - nite! Three-fold let our prai-ses be,

Great mys - te - rious One, to Thee! Un - di - vi - ded Tri - ni - ty! A - men.

Note: This score "Havergal" was William Henry Havergal's next-to-last score. His last score was a musical palindrome on the words "Messiah, Redeemer!" These two scores were composed on his last full day of consciousness, Saturday, April 16, 1870, the day before Easter. See page xii of this book.

No. 164. · **Calvary.** 10 lines 7s, or 77, 77, D.*   [125]

W. H. H., 1869.

Bound up - on th'ac - cur - sed   tree, Faint and bleed-ing, who is   He?   By the

eyes so pale and dim, Streaming blood and writhing limb,   By   the flesh with scourges torn,

By the crown of twis - ted   thorn, By the side so deep - ly pierc'd, By the baf - fled

burn - ing thirst,   By   the drooping, death-dew'd brow, Son of Man, 'tis Thou, 'tis Thou!

* For **77, 77, D,** omit 8th and 9th strains.

[126]

No. 165.   **Gozan.** (*River of*)   **77, 87.**

W. H. H., 1849.

Thou God of grace, our Fa - ther, We now re - joice be - fore Thee;

Thy children we, And lov'd by Thee, 'Tis meet we should a - dore Thee! A - men.

No. 166.   **Zoan II.**   **77, 87** D.

W. H. H., 1845.

Head of Thy Church tri - um-phant. We joy - ful - ly a dore Thee; Till Thou ap - pear, Thy

members here Shall sing like those in glo - ry. We lift our hearts and voi - ces With blest an-

[127]

- ti - ci - pa - tion, And cry a-loud and give to God The praise of our sal - va - tion. A-men.

No. 167.   **Salmon.** (*Hill of*) 78, 78.

W. H. H.

Je - sus lives! no lon - ger now Can thy ter - rors, Death, ap -

- pal us; Je - sus lives! by this we know Thou, O Grave, canst not en -

thral us. Al - le - lu - ia, Al - le - lu - ia! A - men.

н

No. 168.   **Stephanas.**   83, 83, 888, 33.   [128]

F. R. H., 1870.

My heart is fixed, e - ter - nal God, Fixed on Thee; And

my im - mor - tal choice is made, Christ for me! He is my

Pro-phet, Priest, and King, Who did for me sal - va - tion bring, And while I

live I mean to sing, Christ for me. Christ for me! A - men.

No. 169. **Tiberias.** (*SEA OF*) 84, 84, 888, 4

[129]

W. H. H., 1869.

Through the love of God our Sa-viour, All will be well;

Free and change-less is His fa-vour, All, all is well. Pre-cious

is the blood that heal'd us; Per-fect is the grace that seal'd us;

Strong the hand stretch'd out to shield us; All must.......... be well. A-men.

No. 170. **Casiphia.** (*Sea of*) 84, 84, 888, 4. [130]

W. H. H., 1868.

God, that ma - dest earth and hea - ven, Dark - ness and light;

Who the day for toil hast gi - ven, For rest the night;

May Thine an - gel guards de - fend us! Slum - ber sweet Thy mer - cy send us!

Ho - ly dreams and hopes at - tend us, This live - long night! A - men.

No. 171.   **Prague.** 85, 85; or, 85, 83.   [131]

OLD CHURCH PSALMODY.

Thou   who   on   that   won - drous   jour - ney   Sett'st   Thy

face   to   die,   By   Thy   ho - ly,   meek   ex - am - ple,

The last strain thus for 85, 83.

Teach   us   cha - ri - ty!   A - men.

No. 172.   Zared E.   85, 85, 777, 5.   [132]

W. H. H., 1849.

Je - sus from the skies de - scend - ing; Lies a Babe on earth!

Se - raphs o'er the man - ger bend - ing, Hail the won - drous birth!

Lo! the watch - ful shep-herds hear Sounds of joy with ho - ly fear:

Haste to gaze, then, far and near, Spread the ti - - dings forth.

No. 173.   **Zared II.** (*Valley of*)   85, 85, 843.   [133]

W. H. H., 1849.

An - gel voi - ces e - ver sing - ing, Round Thy

throne of light, An - gel harps for e - ver ring - ing,

Rest not day nor night; We would join with them to bless Thee,

And con - fess Thee, Lord of might. A - men.

No. 174.   **Bethany.**   86,84.   [134]

W. H. H., Feb. 1870.

Our blest Re - deem - er, ere He breathed His ten - der last fare - well,

A Guide, a Com - for - ter, be - queathed With us . . . to dwell. A - men.

No. 175.   **Midian.**   86,86,4, or C.M.

W. H. H., 1861.

Re - turn, O wan - d'rer, to thy home, Thy Fa - ther calls for thee; No

lon - ger now an ex - ile roam In guilt and mis - e - - ry. Re - turn! Re - turn!

No. 176.   **Silvanus.**   86,86,86.   [135]

F. R. H., 1872

Fa - ther, I know that all my life Is por - tioned

out for me; The chan - ges that must sure - ly come, I

do not fear to see. But I ask Thee for a

pre - sent mind, In - tent on pleas - ing Thee. A - men.

No. 177.   **Lebanon.**   86,86,88.*   [136]

W. H. H.

Lord, when be - fore Thy throne we meet, Thy good - ness

to a - dore; From heav'n, th' e - ter - nal mer - cy seat, On

us Thy bless - ing pour: And make our in - most souls to

be A ha - bi - ta - tion fit for Thee. A - men.

* For 76, 76, 88, slur 6th and 7th notes of 1st and 3rd strains.

No. 178.   **Sirah.** *(WELL OF)* 87,87.

[137]

W. H. H. cir. 1827.

Soon the trum-pet of sal - - va - tion, Loud - ly, sweet - ly shall be blown;

And each kindred, tongue and na - tion, Shall the thrill-ing man-date own.   A - men.

No. 179.   **Sitnah.** *(WELL OF)* 87,87.

W. H. H., 1842.

Hark! what mean those ho - ly voi-ces, Sweet-ly sounding thro' the skies; Lo! th'an-ge-lic

host re - joi-ces: Heav'nly hal - le - lu-jahs rise. Hal-le - lu -jah! Hal-le - lu-jah! A - men.

No. 177.   **Lebanon.** 86,86,88.*   [138]

W. H. H.

Lord, when be - fore Thy throne we meet, Thy good - ness

to a - dore; From heav'n, th' e - ter - nal mer - cy seat, On

us Thy bless - ing pour: And make our in - most souls to

be A ha - bi - ta - tion fit for Thee. A - men.

* For 76, 76, 88, slur 6th and 7th notes of 1st and 3rd strains.

No. 178.   **Sirah.** (*WELL OF*) 87,87.   [139]

W. H. H. cir. 1827.

Soon the trum-pet of sal - - va - tion, Loud - ly, sweet - ly shall be blown;

And each kindred, tongue and na - tion, Shall the thrill-ing man-date own. A - men.

No. 179.   **Sitnah.** (*WELL OF*) 87,87.

W. H. H., 1842.

Hark! what mean those ho - ly voi - ces, Sweet-ly sounding thro' the skies ; Lo! th'an-ge-lic

host re - joi - ces: Heav'nly hal - le - lu-jahs rise. Hal - le - lu - jah! Hal - le - lu - jah! A - men.

No. 181. **Culbach.** 87,87. [141]

OLD CHURCH PSALMODY.

Praise the Lord ; ye heav'ns a - dore Him ; Praise Him, an - gels, in the height ;

Sun and moon, re-joice be - fore Him ; Praise Him, all ye stars of light. A - men.

No. 182. **Stuttgard.** 87,87.

OLD CHURCH PSALMODY.

Hal - le - - lu - jah! Lord, our voi - ces Rise in cho - ral strains to Thee ;

Son of Man! Thy Church re - joi - ces In her week - ly ju - bi - lee. A - men.

No. 180.   Sirion. (Mount) 87,87.   [140]

W. H. H., 1851.

Hark! ten thou - sand voi - ces cry - ing, "Lamb of

God!" with one ac - cord, Thou - sand thou - sand saints re -

- ply - ing, Wake at once the echo - ing chord.

Hal - - le - lu - jah, Hal - le - lu - jah. A - men.

No. 183. **Frankfort.** 87,87.

OLD CHURCH PSALMODY.

Is - rael's Shepherd, guide me, feed me, Through my pil - grim-age be - low,

And be - side the wa - ters lead me, Where Thy flocks re - joic - ing go. A - men.

No. 184. **Sorek.** (*Valley of*) 87,87.

W. H. H.

Sweet the mo-ments, rich in bless - ing, Which be - fore the cross I spend;

Life and health, and peace pos - sess-ing, From the sin - ner's dy - ing Friend.

No. 185. **Godesberg.*** 87,87.

OLD CHURCH PSALMODY.

Je - sus calls us o'er the tu - mult Of our life's wild rest - less sea;

Day by day His sweet voice sound- eth, Say - ing, Chris-tian, fol - low Me.

No. 186. **Bremen.†** 87,87.

OLD CHURCH PSALMODY.

Shall this life of mine be wast - ed? Shall this vine - yard lie un - till'd?

Shall true joy pass by un - tast - ed, And this soul re - main un - -fill'd?

* Wrongly called WALTHAM or FORTON.   † Wrongly called COBURG.

No. 187.   **Persis.** 87,87,3; or, 87,87.

F. R. H., 1870.

[144]

Lord, I hear of show'rs of bless-ing, Thou art scat-t'ring full and free;

Show'rs the thirst-y land re-fresh-ing; Let some droppings fall on me, Ev-en me. A-men.

No. 188.   **Baden I;** OR, NUREMBERG. 87,87,44,88.

What-e'er my God or-dains is right, Ho-ly His will a - bid - eth;}
I will be still what-e'er He doth, And fol-low where He guid - eth.} He is my God;

Tho' dark my road; He holds me that I shall not fall, Wherefore to Him I leave it all.

No. 189.   **Succoth.** (*Valley of*)   87,87,77.   [145]

W. H. H.

One there is a-bove all o-thers, Well de-serves the name of Friend;

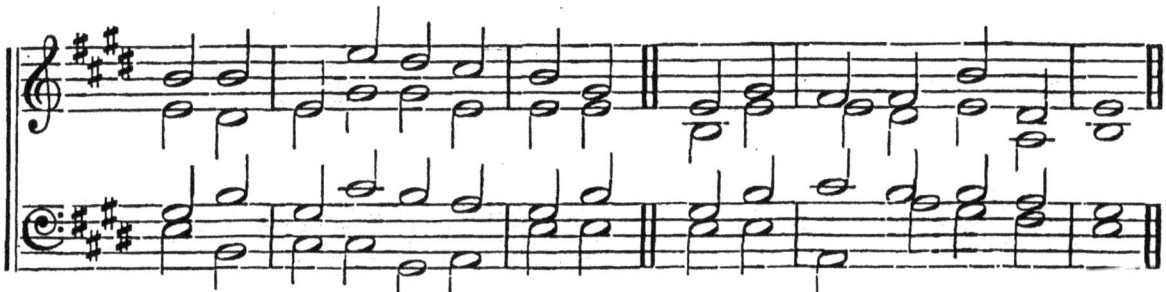

His is love be-yond a bro-ther's, Cost-ly, free, and knows no end.

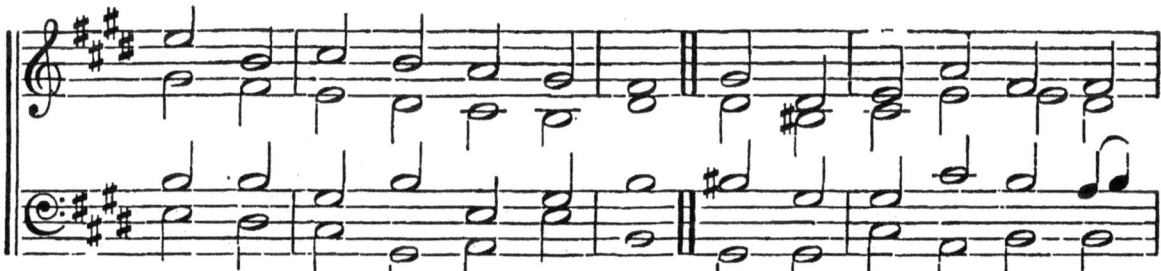

They who once His kind-ness prove, Find it e-ver-last-ing

Hal--le--lu--jah! Hal--le---lu--jah!   A-men.

love.   Hal------le--lu--jah.   1

No. 190.　　　　**Cassel.**　87,87,77.

[14]

OLD CHURCH PSALMODY.

Through the day Thy love has spared us,　Wea - ried we lie

down to rest; Through the si - - lent watch - es guard us,

Let no foe our peace mo - - lest: Je - - sus, Thou our

Guar - dian be; Sweet it is to trust in Thee. A - men.

No. 191. Zaanaim. (PLAIN OF) 87,87,87; or, 87,87,447. [147]

W. H. H., 1849.

Glo - ry, glo - ry e - ver - last - ing Be to Him who

bore the cross; Who re - deem'd our souls by tast - ing

Death, the death de - serv'd by us. Spread His glo - ry,

Spread His glo - ry, Who re - deem'd His peo - ple thus. A - men.

No. 192. **Havilah.** 8͡7,87,87; or, 87,87,447. [148]

W. H. H., Jan. 1870.

Bright - er than me - ri - dian splen - dour, Beams Mes -

- si - ah's spot - less fame; Him we hail our firm De -

- fen - der Him let ev' - ry tongue pro - claim. He is pre - cious,

He is gra - cious, He for e - ver is the same.

No. 193.   **Idumea.**   87,87,87; or, 87,87,447.   [149]

W. H. H. 1866.

An - gels, from the realms of glo - ry, Wing your

flight o'er all the earth, Ye who sang Cre - a - tion's

sto - ry, Now pro - claim Mes - si - ah's birth: Come and wor - ship,

Come and wor - ship, Wor - ship Christ the new - born King.

No. 194.   𝕿𝖊𝖒𝖆𝖓.   87,87,87; or 87,87,447.   [160]

W. H. H., 1869.

To the Name of our sal - va - tion Laud and

hon - our let us pay; Which for many a gen - er - a - tion

Hid in God's fore - know-ledge lay, But with ho - ly ex - ul -

- ta - tion We may sing a - loud to - day.   A - men

No. 195.   **Media.**   87,87,87; or, 87,87,447.   [151]

W. H. H., 1859.

Guide me, O Thou great Je - ho - vah, Pil - grim

through this bar - ren land, I am weak, but Thou art migh - ty;

Hold me with Thy pow'r - ful hand; Bread of hea - ven, Bread of

hea - ven, Feed me now and ev - er more. A - men.

No. 196.   **Coburg.**   87,87,87 ; or, 87,87,447.   [152]

OLD CHURCH PSALMODY.

Lo! He comes with clouds de - scend - ing, Once for

fa - vour'd sin - ners slain. Thou - sand thou - sand saints at - tend - ing,

Swell the tri - umph of His train: Hal - le - lu - jah!

Hal - le - lu - jah! God ap - pears on earth to reign. A - men.

No. 197. **Tabor.** (*Mount*) 87,87,447. [153]

W. H. H.

Day of judg-ment! day of won-ders! Hark, the

trum-pet's aw-ful sound, Lou-der than a thou-sand thun-ders,

Shakes the vast cre - a - tion round! How the sum-mons,

How the sum-mons Will the sin-ner's heart con-found!

No. 198.   **Ulai.** *(River)* 87,87,447.   [154]

W. H. H.

Wide - ly, 'midst the slum - b'ring na - tions, Dark - ness

holds his des - pot sway; Cru - el in his ha - bi - ta - tions,

Ruth - less o'er his pro - strate prey. Star of Beth - lehem,

Star of Beth-lehem, Rise and beam in con - qu'ring day! A - men.

No. 199.   **Lusatia.** 87,87,447.   [155]

OLD CHURCH PSALMODY.

Lead us, heav'n - ly Fa - ther! lead us O'er the

world's tem - pes - tuous sea; Guard us, guide us, keep us, feed us,

For we have no help but Thee: Yet pos - sess - ing

ev' - ry bless - ing, If our God our Fa - ther be. A - men.

No. 200. **Tekoa.** (*WILDERNESS OF*) 87,87,447. [156]

W. H. H., 1852.

Art Thou, Lord, re - buk - ing na - tions? Hast Thou

bared Thy glit- t'ring sword? War and death's dread de - vas - ta - tions,

Are they march - ing at Thy word? Shield us, Sa - viour,

With Thy fa - vour, When Thy vi - als are out - pour'd. A - men.

No. 201.   **Shen.** (*THE ROCK*)   87,87 D.*   [157]

W. H. H., 1853.

Hal - le - lu - jah! Hal - le - lu - jah! Hearts to heav'n and voi - ces raise;

Sing to God a hymn of glad-ness, Sing to God a hymn of praise. He who

on the cross a Vic - tim For the world's sal - va - tion bled, Je - sus

Christ, the King of Glo - ry, Now is ris - en from the dead. A - men.

* For 12 lines 87, repeat 1st, 2nd, 7th, and 8th strains.

No. 202.   𝕰𝖘𝖉𝖗𝖆𝖊𝖑𝖔𝖓.   87,87 D.   [158]

(See Preface, p. xxi.)

W. H. H., cir. 1838.

Come, Thou Fount of ev' - ry bless - ing, Tune my heart to sing Thy grace,

Streams of mer - cy, ne - ver ceas - ing, Call for songs of loud - est praise.

Teach me some me - lo - dious mea - sure Sung by flam - ing hosts a - bove;

Fill my soul with sa - cred plea - sure, While I sing re - deem - ing love. A - men.

No. 203.   **Salzburg.***   87,87 D.   [159]

(See Preface, p. xxi.)

OLD CHURCH PSALMODY.

Glo - rious things of Thee are spo - ken; Zi - on, ci - ty of our God;

He whose word can - not be bro - ken, Form'd thee for His own a - bode.

On the Rock of A - ges found-ed, What can shake thy sure re - pose?

With sal - va-tion's walls sur - round-ed, Thou may'st smile at all thy foes.

* Wrongly called BENEDICTION or ST. WERBERGH.

No. 204.   **Shinar.** (*Plain*) 87,87 D.   [60]

W. H. H., 1868.

Hail, thou once de-spis-ed Je-sus, Hail thou Ga-li-le-an King:

Thou didst suf-fer to re-lease us, Thou didst free sal-va-tion bring.

Hail, thou ag-on-iz-ing Sav-iour, Bear-er of our sin and shame,

By Thy mer-its we find fa-vour; Life is giv-en thro' Thy Name. A-men.

No. 205.   **Hamburg.**   87,87 D.   [161]

OLD CHURCH PSALMODY.

Je - sus, I my cross have tak - en, All to leave and fol - low Thee;

Des - ti - tute, de - spis'd, for - sak - en, Thou from hence my all shalt be;

Pe - rish ev' - ry fond am - bi - tion, All I've sought, or hoped, or known;

Yet how rich is my con - di - tion! God and heav'n are still my own. A - men.

No. 206   **Augsburg.**   87,87 D.   [162]

OLD CHURCH PSALMODY.

Dread Je - ho - vah, God of na - tions, From Thy tem - ple in the skies,

Hear Thy peo - ple's sup - pli - ca - tions, Now for their de - liv'- rance rise,

Lo, with deep con - tri - tion turn - ing, Hum - bly at Thy feet we bend;

Hear us fast - ing, pray - ing, mourn - ing; Hear us, spare us, and de - fend. A - men.

No. 207.   **Zoheleth.**   (STONE OF)   87,87,887.   [163]

W. H. H., cir. 1858.

The Lord   of   Might from   Si - nai's   brow, Gave   forth   His   voice   of

thun - der;   And   Is - rael   lay   on   earth be - low,   Out - stretch'd in

fear   and   won - der.   Be - neath His   feet   was   pitch - y   night, And

at   His   left   hand   and   His right,   The   rocks were rent a - sun - der.

[164]

No. 208.   **Altorf.** (LUTHER'S HYMN, so called) 87,87,887 ; or 88,888.

(See Preface, p. xxi.)   OLD CHURCH PSALMODY.

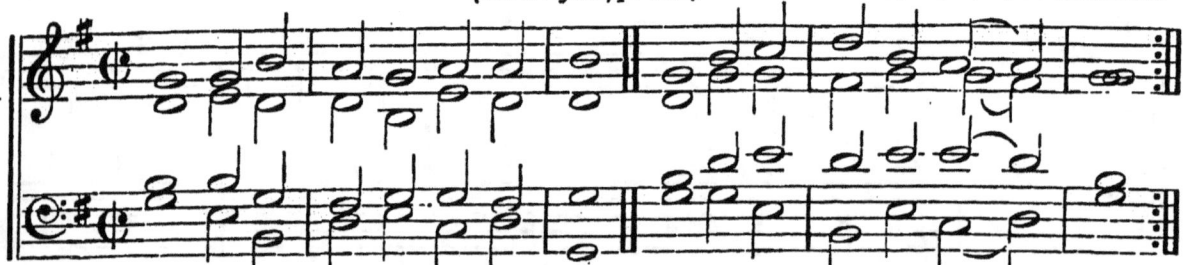

Great God, what do I see and hear ? The end of things cre - a - - ted :
The Judge of all men doth ap - pear On clouds of glo - ry sea - - ted :

The trum - pet sounds, the graves re - store The dead which they con-

- tain'd be - fore ; Pre - pare, my soul, to meet Him. A - men.

No. 209.   **Tryphosa.**   886.

F. R. II., 1870.

To Him, Who for our sins was slain, To Him, for all His dy - ing pain,

TRYPHOSA—*continued.*

[165]

Sing we Al - le - lu ia,   Al - le - lu - ia,   Al - le - lu - ia !   A - men.

No. 210.   **Magdalene College.***   886 D.

OLD CHURCH PSALMODY.

Come, see the   place where Je - sus   lay,   And hear an - gel - ic watchers

say,   He lives who once was slain: Why seek the liv - ing 'midst the dead?

Re - mem - ber how the Sa - viour said   That He would rise a - gain.   A - men.

* Wrongly called ST. JUDE, or KINGSTON, or PADERBORN.

No. 211. **Jordan.** 886 D. [166]

W. H. H., 1851.

Let Zi - on in her songs re - cord The ho - nours

of her dy - ing Lord, Tri - um - phant o - ver sin;

How sweet the song there's none can say, But he whose

sins are wash'd a - way, Who feels the same with - in.

No. 212.   **New College.** 886 D.

OLD CHURCH PSALMODY.

Love,   on - ly   love, Thy heart in - clin'd,   And brought Thee,

Sa - viour of man - kind, Down   from   Thy throne a - bove;

Love made Thee here a man of grief,   Thy   vi - sage

marr'd for my re - lief;   O   mys - te - ry of love!

No. 213.   **Kedron.** (BROOK)   886 D.*   [168]

W. H. H.

O love Di - vine, how sweet Thou art! When shall I

find my wil - ling heart All ta - ken up by Thee?

I thirst, I faint, I die to prove The great - ness

of re - deem - ing love, The love of Christ to me! A - men.

* For 884 D, omit the notes in [ ].

No. 214.   **Chapel Royal.**   886 D.†   [169]

OLD CHURCH PSALMODY.

From whence this fear and un - be - lief? Hath not the

Fa - ther put to grief His spot - less Son for me?

And will the right - eous Judge of men Con - demn me

for that debt of sin Which, Lord, was charged on Thee?

* Wrongly called OXFORD, or HEREFORD, or BROADMEAD.
† For 8888, 6, omit the 3rd strain.

No. 215. **Merom.** (*Waters of*) 887, 887. [170]

W. H. H., 1857.

In Thy glo - rious Re - sur - rec - tion, Lord, we see a

world's e - rec - tion, Man in Thee is glo - ri - fied;

Bliss for which the Pa - triarchs pant - ed, Joys by ho - ly

psalm - ists chant - ed, Now in Thee are ve - ri - fied

No 216.   **Chaldea.** 888.   [171]

W. H. H., cir. 1835.

O sons and daughters, let us sing! The King of Heav'n, the glorious King,

O'er death to-day rose tri-um-phing. Al-le-lu-ia! A-men.

No. 217.   **Tryphena.** 888.

F. R. H., 1870.

Ac-cept-ed, per-fect, and com-plete! For God's in-he-ri-

-tance made meet; How true, how glo-rious, and how sweet! A-men.

No. 218. **Dies Irae.** 888.* [172]

(PART I.)

F. R. H., 1870.

Day of wrath, O day of mourn-ing! See the Cru - ci -

fied re - turn - ing, Heav'n and earth in ash - es burn - ing!

(PART II.)

Think, kind Je - su, my sal - va - tion Caused Thy won - drous

in - car - na - tion: Leave me not to de - so - la - tion.

* Part I. is to be sung to the first eight triplets of "Day of wrath, O day of mourning." Part II. begins at "Think, kind Jesu, my salvation." Part III. begins at "Ah! that day of tears and mourning," and closes.

(PART III.)   [173]

Ah, that day of tears and mourn - ing! From the dust of

earth re - turn - ing, Man for judg - ment must pre - pare him;

Spare, O God, in mer - cy spare him. Lord, all pi - tying,

rall.

Je - su blest. Grant us Thine e - ter - nal rest. A - men.

No. 219.   **Carpus.**   888, 4.   [174]

F. R. H., 1870.

Hope, Christian soul; in ev'-ry stage   Of this thine earth-ly pil-grim-age,

Let heav'n-ly joy thy thoughts en-gage: A-bound.. in hope.

No. 220.   **Jezreel.** (*Valley of*)   888, 4.

W. H. H., cir. 1857.

My God, my Fa-ther, while I stray   Far from my home in life's rough way;

O teach me from my heart to say, "Thy will be done!" A-men.

No. 221. **Eshcol.** (*Valley & Brook*) 888, 6. [175]

W. H. H., 1852.

O ho - ly Sa-viour, Friend un-seen! The faint, the weak may on Thee lean;

Help me, through-out life's va-rying scene, By faith to cling to Thee. A - men.

No. 222. **Bethabara E.**; or, Hatherton. 888, 6.

W. H. H., 1860.

Just as I am, with-out one plea, But that Thy blood was shed for me,

And that Thou bid'st me come to Thee, O Lamb of God, I come.

Bethabara II. 888, 6.   (MAJOR.)   [176]

Just as thou art, with-out one trace   Of love, or joy, or in-ward grace,

Or meetness for the heav'n-ly place,   O guil-ty sin-ner, come!

No. 223.   **Philemon.** 888, 7.

F. R. H., 1870.

Bring   to   Christ   your   best   o - bla - tion,   Grate - ful

hearts, and a - do - ra - tion,   Join   in   songs   of   gra - tu -

[177]

. . la - tion, Chris - tian peo - ple, on this day. A - men.

No. 224.   **Aristarchus.**   88, 88.

F. R. H., 1870.

In - spi - rer and Hear - er of pray'r, Thou Shep - herd and

Guar - dian of Thine, My all to Thy co - ve - nant care

I sleep - ing and wa - king, re - sign. A - - men

L

No. 225. **Baden II**; OR, NUREMBERG.* 88, 88, 47. [178]

OLD CHURCH PSALMODY.

Ho - san - na to the li - ving Lord: Ho - san - na

to th' In - car - nate Word! To Christ, Cre - a - tor, Sa - viour,

King, Let earth, let heav'n, Ho - san - na sing: Ho - san - na,

Lord; Ho - san - na in the high - est! A - men.

* So arranged as to suit those versions of the Hymn which omit the " Hosanna, Lord."

No. 226.   𝕸𝖆𝖒𝖗𝖊. (*PLAIN OF*)   88, 88, 88.*

[179]

W. H. H.

We sing His love, who once was slain, Who soon o'er

death re-vived a-gain, That all His saints through Him might have

E - ter-nal con-quest o'er the grave. Soon shall the trum-pet

sound, and we Shall rise to im-mor-tal- i - ty. A - men.

* For 98, 98, 88, repeat last note of 1st and 3rd strains.

No. 227.   𝔄𝔫𝔤𝔢𝔩𝔰' 𝔖𝔬𝔫𝔤.   88, 88, 88; or, L.M.   [180]
                            (See Preface, p. xxii.)
                                                        OLD CHURCH PSALMODY.

Cre - a - tor   Spi - rit!   by whose   aid   The world's foun -

- da - tions first were laid,   Come, vi - sit ev' - ry hum - ble mind,

And pour Thy joy on all man - kind: From sin and sor - row

set us free,   And make us tem - ples meet for Thee.   A - men.

No. 228. **Meribah.** (ROCK OF) 88, 88, 88; or, 10 6, 10 6, 884.*

[181]

W. H. H.

Thou hid - den love of God, whose height, Whose depth un -

fa - thom'd, no man knows: I see from far Thy beau - teous

light, And in - ly sigh for Thy re - pose: My heart is pain'd, nor

can it be At rest till it find rest in Thee. A - men.

* For 10 6, 10 6, 884, repeat last four notes.

No. 229.   **Maon.** (*Wilderness of*)   88, 88, 88.   [182]

W. H. H.

The Lord my pas - ture shall pre - pare, And feed me

with a Shep-herd's care; His pre - sence shall my wants sup -

ply, And guard me with a watch - ful eye; My noon - day

walks He will at - tend, And all my mid - night hours de - fend.

No. 230.   Exeter.   888 D.   [183]

OLD CHURCH PSALMODY.

Oh ! for a burst of praise to God, Who bought His Church with His own

blood, And will His dear-bought right maintain; Soon shall His voice dis - pel our

gloom The mar - riage of the Lamb is come, To crown His bride, with

Him to reign.   Al - le - lu - ia, Al - le - lu - ia!   A - men.

No. 231. **Capernaum.** 98, 98. [184]

W. H. H., 1860.

Bread of the world, in mer-cy bro-ken; Wine of the soul, in mer-cy shed;

By whom the words of life were spo-ken, And in whose death our sins are dead. A - men.

No. 232. **Aquila.** 9998, 8888.

F. R. H. 1870.

I will go in the strength of the Lord, In the path He hath mark'd for my feet;

I will fol-low the light of His word, Nor shrink from the dan-gers I meet;

[185]

His pre - sence my steps shall at - tend, His ful - ness my wants shall sup - ply;

On Him till my jour - ney shall end, My hope shall se - cure - ly re - ly.

No. 233.   **Gedor.**   10, 10, 7.

W. H. H., 1867.

Sing Al - le - lu - ia forth in du - teous praise, O ci - ti - zens of

heav'n: in sweet notes raise An end - less Al - le - lu - ia! A - men.

No. 234.   **Conway.**   10 10, 10 10.   [186]

OLD CHURCH PSALMODY.

"Je - ho - vah E - lo - him!" Cre - a - tor Great,

Who art with glo - rious at - tri - butes ar - ray'd;

To Thee by heav'n and earth and all there - in,

Be e - ver - last - ing praise and wor - ship paid. A - men.

No 235.   **Ophir.**   10 10, 10 10.   [187]

W. H. H., 1867.

A - bide   with   me, . . .   fast   falls   the   e - ven - tide;

The   dark - ness   deep - ens;   Lord,   with   me   a - - bide:

When   o - - ther   help - - ers   fail,   and   com - forts   flee,

rall. . . . . .

Help   of   the   help - less,   O   a - bide   with   me.   A - men.

No. 236.   **Ebronah.**   10 10, 10 10.   [188]

W. H. H., 1867.

I jour - ney through a de - sert drear and wild,

Yet is my heart by such sweet thoughts be - guil'd,

Of Him on whom I lean, my Strength, my Stay,

I can for - get the sor - rows of the way. A-men.

No. 237. **Old cxxivth.*** IO IO IO, IO IO. [189]

OLD CHURCH PSALMODY.

Our year of grace is wear - ing to its close, Its au - tumn

storms are low'r - ing from the sky : Shine on us with Thy

light, O God Most High : A - bide with us wher - e'er our path - way goes,

Our Guide in toil, our Guar - dian in re - pose. A - men.

* Wrongly called BASLE or MONTAGUE.

No. 238.   **Zemaraim.** (*Mount*)   10·10, 10 10, 10 10.*   [190]

W. H. H., 1867.

Chris-tians, a - wake!... sa - lute the hap - py morn, Where - on the Sa-viour

of man - kind   was   born; Rise to a - dore the mys - te - ry   of   love,

Which hosts of an - gels chant - ed from a - bove; With them the joy - ful ti - dings

first be - gun Of God In - car - nate and the Vir - gin's Son. A - men.

* For 10 10, 10 10, omit 3rd and 4th strains.

No. 239.   **Hanover;** or, MODERN CIVth.   10 10, 11 11.   [191]

See Preface, p. xxii.   OLD CHURCH PSALMODY.

By an - gels in heav'n of ev' - ry de - gree,

And saints up - on earth all praise be ad - drest,

To God in three Per - sons, one God e - ver blest,

As it has been, now is, and al - ways shall be. A - men.

No. 240.   **Ripon.**   10 10, 11 11.

OLD CHURCH PSALMODY.

[192]

Ye ser-vants of God, Your Mas - ter pro - claim,

And pub - lish a - broad His won - der - ful name.

The name all - vic - to - rious Of Je - sus ex - tol;

His king - dom is glo - rious, And rules o - ver all.

No. 241. **Paran.** (*WILDERNESS OF*) 10 10, 11 11; or, 11 11, 11 11. [193]

W. H. H.

O wor - ship the King, all glo - rious a - bove;

O grate - ful - ly sing His pow'r and His love!

Our Shield and De - fend - er, the An - cient of Days,

Pa - vi - lion'd in splen-dour and gird - ed with praise. A - men.

No. 242.   **Peor.** (*Mount*)   10 10, 10 10; or, 11 11, 11 11.

W. H. H.

The night is far spent, the day is at hand;

Al - rea - dy the dawn may be seen in the sky;

Re - joice then, ye saints, 'tis your Lord's own com - mand;

Re - joice, for the coming of Je - sus draws nigh.

No. 243.   **Sosthenes.**   10 11, 11 11, 12 11.*

F. R. H., 1870.

Sound the loud tim-brel o'er E-gypt's dark sea, Je - ho-vah hath triumph'd, His

peo - ple are free! Sing, for the pride of the ty - rant is bro-ken:

His chariots and horsemen, all splen-did and brave, How vain was their boasting, the

Lord hath but spo - ken, And chariots and horse-men are sunk in the wave.

* For 8 lines, D.C. 1st and 2nd strains.

No. 244. **Crescens.** 11 8, 11 8.

F. R. H., 1870.

In songs of su - blime a - do - ra - tion and praise,

Ye pil - grims to Si - on who press, Break

forth, and ex - tol the great An - cient of Days, His

rich and dis - tin - guish - ing grace. A - - - men.

No. 245.   **Sternberg.**   11 10, 11 10.

OLD CHURCH PSALMODY.

Bright - est and best of the sons of the morn - ing,

Dawn   on   our   dark - ness,   and   lend   us   Thine   aid ;

Star   of   the   East,   the   ho - ri - zon   a - dorn - ing,

Guide where our In - fant Re - deem - er is laid.

[197]

No. 246.   **Eirene.**   11 10, 11 10.   [198]

F. R. H., 1870.

Fa - ther, whose hand.... hath led me so se - cure - ly;

Fa - ther, whose ear hath lis-ten'd to my pray'r; Fa - ther, whose eye...... hath

watch'd o'er me so sure - ly,   Whose heart hath lov'd me with a

For 11 10, 11 10, 10 12, the two strains following may be added.*

love so rare.

* For 11 10, 11 10, 10 10, omit the notes in [ ]

[199]

A-men.

No. 247. **Candia.** 11, 11, 11, 5.

W. H. H.

Lord of our life, and God of our sal - va - tion, Star of our

night,...... and Hope of ev' - ry na - tion, Hear and re - ceive........ Thy

church's sup - pli - ca - tion, Lord God Al - migh - ty. A - men.

No. 248.   **Hobah.**   11 11, 11 11.   [200]

W H. H., 1846.

The Church of our fa - thers! so dear to our souls;

Ay, dear as the life - blood with - in us that rolls!

We'll ral - ly a - round her by dan - gers un - aw'd,

The Church of our fa - thers! the Church of our God!

No. 249.　　　　　**Trisagion.** 11 12, 12 10.　　　　[201]

W. H. H., 1852.

Ho - ly, ho - ly, ho - ly! Lord .. God Al - migh - ty!

Ear - ly in the morn - ing our song shall rise to Thee;

1st and 4th verses.　　　　2nd and 3rd verses.

Che - ru - bim and Se - ra - phim
On - ly Thou art Ho - ly,

Ho - ly, ho - ly, ho - ly!　　　　　Mer - ci -

- ful and migh - ty, God in Three Per - sons, Bless - ed Tri - ni - ty. A - men.

No. 250.   **Venite Adoremus.**   12 10, 11 10.   [202]

W. H. H., 1860.

O come, all ye faith - ful, joy - ful - ly tri - um - phant; To

Beth - le - hem haste ye with glad . . . ac - cord; Lo! in a

man - ger lies the King of an - gels; O come, let us a - dore Him, O come, let

us a - dore Him, O come, let us a - dore Him, Christ the Lord. A - men.

No. 251.   " Nun danket alle Gott."   67,67,6666.   [203]

(*See Preface, p.* xxiii.)

Now thank we all our God, With heart and hand and voi - ces,

Who won-drous things hath done, In whom His world re - joic - - es.

Who from our mo-ther's arms, Hath bless'd us on our way,

With couut-less gifts of love, And still is ours to-day. A-men.

No. 252. **"Ein' feste Burg ist unser Gott."** 87,87,6666,7. [204]

(*See Preface, p. xxiii.*)

Re - joice to - day with one ac - cord, Sing out with
Re - joice and praise our migh - ty Lord, Whose arm hath

ex - ul - ta - - tion; }
brought sal - va - - tion; } His works of love pro - claim The great-ness

of His name; For He is God a - lone. Who hath His

mer - cy shown; Let all His saints a - dore... Him. A men.

No. 253. St. Paul. 87,887,77,77. [205]

(*See Preface, p.* xxiii.)

F. R. H. 1871.

Wor-thy of all a - do - ra - tion Is the Lamb that once was slain! Cry, in

rap-tured ex - ul - ta - tion, His redeemed from ev' - ry na-tion, An-gel myriads

join the strain. Sounding from their sin - less strings Glo - ry to the King of kings;

Harp - ing with their harps of gold, Praise which ne - ver can be told. A - men.

HYMN CHANTS.   [206]

No. I.   **Worcester Chant.**   (RECTE ET RETRO.)

W. H. H., c. 1834.

O God of Hosts, the migh - ty Lord, How love - ly is the place

Where Thou, enthron'd in glo - ry, shew'st The bright - ness of Thy face.

No. II.   **Ephesus.**   (UNISON.)

W. H. H., c. 1836.

This is the day the Lord hath made, He calls the hours His own;

Let heaven rejoice, let earth be glad, And praise sur - round the throne.

No. III.   **Smyrna.** (DOUBLE COUNTERPOINT.)   [207]

W. H. H., c. 1836.

O God, our help in á - ges past, Our hópe for years to come,

Our shelter from the stór - my blast, And óur e - ter - nal home.

No. IV.   **Pergamos.**

F. R. H., 1870.

The strain upraise of jóy and praise, Alle - lú - ia!

To the glory of their King shall the ransomed péo - ple ring, Alle - lú - ia!

No. V.   **Thyatira.**   [208]

F. R. H., 1871.

One sweetly só - lemn thought Comes to me ó'er and o'er,

I am nearer my hóme to - day Than I ever have béen be - fore.

No. VI.   **Sardis.**

F. R. H , 1870.

I thought upon my sins, and I was sad, My soul was troubled sore and fíll'd with pain ;

But then I thought } ánd was glad, My heavy grief } jóy a - gain.
on Jesus   was turned to

* The last line thus if for three syllables only

No. VII. **Philadelphia.** (5 lines.) [209]

F. R. H., 1870.

Come, lá-bour on! Who dares stand idle on the } hár-vest plain, While all around him waves the } góld-en grain?

And to each servant does the Más - ter say, "Go, wórk to - day!"

No. VIII. **Laodicea.** (6 lines.)

F. R. H., 1870.

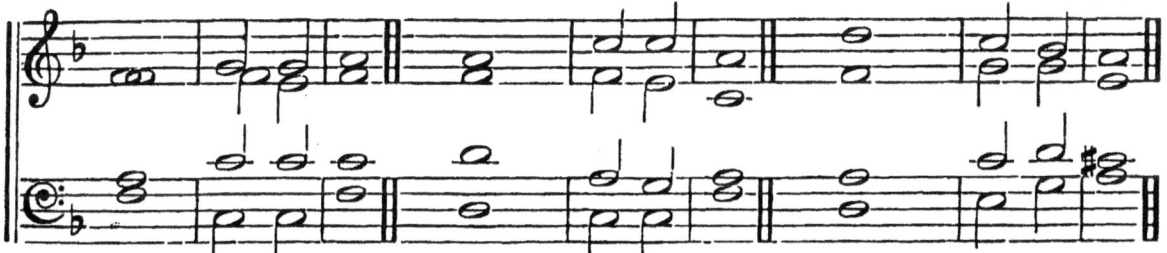

Long did I toil, and knew no } éarth - ly rest, Far did I rove, and found no } cér-tain home, At last I sought them in His } shélt'ring breast,

Who opes His arms, and bids the } wéa-ry come: With Him I found a home, a } rést di - vine, And I since then am His, and } Hé is mine. A-men

Chant Service for the Te Deum. [210]

W. H. H.

We praise Thee, O God, we acknowledge Thee to be the Lord.

When Thou tookest upon Thee to deliver man, Thou didst not abhor the Vir - gin's womb.

Day by day we magni - fy Thee.

Vouchsafe, O Lord, to keep us this day with - -out sin.

[211]

CHANT SERVICE FOR THE TE DEUM—*continued.*

O Lord, in Thee have I trusted; let me ne - ver be con - found - ed.

PSALM CHANTS.*

W. H. H., 1863.

No. I. (Suitable for Psalm ciii.)

No. II. (Psalm cxxi.)

No. III. (Psalm cxxxvi.)

No. IV. (Psalm cxlv.)

No. V. (Psalm xxiii.)

No. VI. (Psalm xx.)

* The initial note of each part of these Chants is intended for the deliberate recitation of all that precedes the last accented syllable of each half of a verse, whether that syllable be the last word, or the last part of a word, or the last word but one. By this method all who can read the Psalms may chant them as easily as they sing a line of a common hymn.

KYRIES.

No. 1.

[2/2]

W. H. H., 1863.

Lord, have mer - cy up - on us,

and in - cline

and in - cline our hearts to keep this law.

Lord, have mer - cy up - on us, and write all

these Thy laws in our hearts, we be - seech Thee.

No. 2.

[213]

W. H. H., 1868.

Lord, have mer - cy up - on us, and in -

- cline our hearts to keep this law.

Lord, have mer - cy up - on us, and write all

these Thy laws in our hearts, we be - seech Thee.

No. 3.

[214]
W. H. H., 1866.

Lord, have mer - cy up - on......... us,

and in - cline our hearts to keep this law.

Lord, have mer - cy up - on....... us, and write all

these Thy laws in our hearts, we be - seech...... Thee.

No. 4.

[215]

W. H. H., 1863.

Lord, have mer - cy up - on us, and in -

cline our hearts to keep this law.

Lord, have mer - cy up - on us, and write all

these Thy laws in our hearts, we be - seech.... Thee

No. 5.

[2/6]

W. H. H., 1867.

Lord, have mer - cy up - on us,

and in - cline our hearts to keep this law.

Lord, have mer - cy up - on us, and write all these Thy

in our hearts,.............

laws   in our hearts, we be - seech...... Thee.

rall.

No. 6.

W. H. H., 1868.

[217]

Lord, have mer - cy up - on......... us,

and in - cline our hearts to keep this law.

Lord, have mer - cy up - on......... us, and write all

these Thy laws in our hearts, we be - seech Thee.

GLORIAS. [218]

No. 1.

W. H. H., 1856.

Glo - ry be................... to Thee, O Lord!

Glo - ry be to Thee, to Thee, O Lord!

Glo - ry be to Thee, O Lord!

No. 2.

W. H. H., 1866.

Glo - ry be to Thee, O Lord!

No. 3.

W. H. H., 1863.

be to Thee, O Lord!

Glo - ry be to Thee, O Lord!

[219]

No. 4.

W. H. H., 1866.

Glo - ry be to Thee, O Lord!...............

No. 5.

W. H. H., 1866.

Glo - ry be to Thee, O Lord!

No. 6

W. H. H., 1866.

Glo - ry be to Thee, O Lord!

Ter Sanctus.   [220]

W. H. H., 1836.

There- fore with an - gels and arch - - - - an - gels,

and with all the com - pa - ny of heav'n, of heav'n,

laud,   We laud,

We laud and mag - ni - fy,   We laud and mag - ni - fy Thy

glo - rious Name ; Ev - er - more prais - - - ing Thee, and

TER SANCTUS—*continued.* [221]

say - ing, Ho - ly, ho - ly, ho - ly, Lord . .

God of hosts, Heav'n and earth are full of Thy . .

glo - ry: Glo - ry be to Thee, to Thee, O

Lord most high. A - men, A - - men.

[222]

525

Thine is the Power.

I

Our Father, our Father! who dwellest in light,
We lean on Thy love & we rest on Thy might;
In weakness & weariness joy shall abound,
For Strength everlasting in Thee shall be found:
Our Refuge, our Helper, in conflict & woe,
Our mighty Defender, - how blessèd to know
That Thine is the That Thine is the Power!

II

Our Father, Thy promise we earnestly claim,

All glory to Thee, our victorious King.
For Thine is the Power

V   VI   IX
Our Father, Thy children rejoice in Thy reign
Rejoice in Thy ~~~~~~ & praise Thee again!
Yea, Thine is the kingdom, & Thine is the might,
And Thine is the glory, transcendently bright:
For ever and ever that glory shall shine,
For ever & ever that kingdom be Thine,
For Thine is the Power!

Frances Ridley Havergal. May 14. 1872.

Very few manuscript scores in F.R.H.'s handwriting have been found (the list is given on page xxvii at the front of this book), but this manuscript was apparently written in the very great, costly, extensive preparation of Songs of Grace and Glory *by her and Rev. Snepp (see pages 499–517 and 402 of Volume V of the Havergal edition). This is the top of the first page of a three-page manuscript in F.R.H.'s handwriting, with also the bottom of the third page. This was hymn number 525* Songs of Grace and Glory *(on page 763 of Volume V).*

Note : This was another blank page in the original book.

II. The Bethlehem Shepherd-Boy's Tale. [223]

A CHRISTMAS CAROL.

W. H. H., 1834.

Moderately fast.

So hap - py all the day, Had I been with - out

play, And such good thoughts had come o'er my mind,

That I won - der'd what it meant, Or for why it was

sent, As I ne'er had felt aught of the kind.

II. The Worcestershire Christmas Carol. [224]

W. H. H., 1827.

How grand and how bright, That

won - der - ful night, When an - gels to Beth - le - hem came! They

burst forth like fires, They struck their gold lyres, And min - gled their

rall.

sound with the flame.

III. The First Anniversary of Christmas. [225]

A CHRISTMAS CAROL.

Joyously and briskly.

W. H. H. 1847.

Come, shep-herds, come, 'tis just a year Since sweet-est mu-sic

woke our ear, And An - gels bless'd our sight. . . . .

Come, lift your heart, and tune your voice, And bid the hills and

vales re-joice, As on that glo - rious night. . .

[226]

This next set of five indices was copied from an earlier—1871—edition of *Havergal's Psalmody and Century of Chants* published by Robert Cocks & Co.:

This section of twenty pages i to xx was followed by an advertisement page in the original Cocks edition. This advertisement page is found on page 1025 of Volume V of the Havergal edition.

Note: This was another blank page in the original book.

I.

INDEX OF TUNES. [227]

(ALPHABETICALLY ARRANGED).

No.	Name.	Measure.	Author or Harmonist.	Date.	Source.
81	Abana	S. M.	W. H. Havergal	1845	Hundred Tunes.
89	Abarim	S. M.	W. H. Havergal	......	Hundred Tunes.
138	Abilene	77, 77	W. H. Havergal	1866	Unpublished MS.
88	Achor	S. M.	W. H. Havergal	1847	Hundred Tunes.
48	Adria	C. M.	W. H. Havergal	1869	Unpublished MS.
86	Ajalon	S. M.	W. H. Havergal	......	Hundred Tunes.
208	Altorf ; or, *Luther's Hymn*	87, 87, 887 ; or, 88, 888	Dr. Martin Luther. From "Winterfeld's Collection, 1840." Harmonized by W. H. H.	1523	Old Church Psalmody.
84	Amana	S. M.	W. H. Havergal	1838	Hundred Tunes.
103	Amplias	64, 66.	F. R. Havergal	1870	
227	Angels' Song	88, 88, 88...	Orlando Gibbons. Harmonized by W. H. H.	1623	Old Church Psalmody.
232	Aquila	9998, 8888...	F. R. Havergal	1870	
224	Aristarchus	8888.	F. R. Havergal	1870	
90	Armageddon	S. M.	W. H. Havergal	1841	Hundred Tunes.
118	Arnon	66, 84	W. H. Havergal. (Adapted, F. R. H.)	1841	Hundred Tunes.
59	Arran	C. M.	W. H. Havergal	1869	Unpublished MS.
206	Augsburg	87, 87 D.	From Töpler's " Alte Choral Melodien." Harmonized by W. H. H.	......	Old Church Psalmody.
79	Aven	S. M.	W. H. Havergal	1841	Hundred Tunes.
116	Baca	66, 66, 66	W. H. Havergal. (Adapted, F. R. H.)	1852	Hundred Tunes.
188	Baden I ; or, *Nuremberg.*	87, 87, 44, 87	Severus Gastorius. Harmonized by W. H. H. (Adapted, F. R. H.)	1675	Old Church Psalmody.
225	Baden II ; or, *Nuremberg.*	88, 88, 47	Severus Gastorius. Harmonized by W. H. H.	1675	Old Church Psalmody.
112	Bashan	66, 66	W. H. Havergal	c 1858	Hundred Tunes.
18	Bavaria	L. M.	Ancient German Choral. Harmonized by W. H. H.	......	Old Church Psalmody.
66	Bedford	C. M.	From "Matthew Wilkins' Psalmody." Harmonized by W. H. H.	1699	Old Church Psalmody.
41	Berachah	C. M.	W. H. Havergal	c1858	Hundred Tunes.
51	Besor	C. M.	W. H. Havergal	1835	Hundred Tunes.
222	Bethabara ; or, *Hatherton*	888, 6	W. H. Havergal	1860	" Year of Praise," &c., &c.
174	Bethany	86, 84	W. H. Havergal	Feb. 1870	Unpublished MS.
76	Bethaven	C. M. D.	W. H. Havergal	c 1857	Hundred Tunes.
36	Bether	C. M.	W. H. Havergal	......	Hundred Tunes.
102	Beulah	64, 64, 6664	W. H. Havergal	c 1866	Unpublished MS.
186	Bremen	87, 87.	Joachim Neander, Presbyter of Bremen. Harmonized by W. H. H.	1680	Old Church Psalmody.
43	Bristol	C. M.	From " Ravenscroft's Psalter." Harmonized by W. H. H.	1621	Old Church Psalmody.

No.	Name.	Measure.	Author or Harmonist.	Date.	Source.
56	Caithness	C. M.	From the " Scotch Psalter." Harmonized by W. H. H.	1635	Old Church Psalmody.
164	Calvary	10 lines 7s or 7777 D. ...	W. H. Havergal. (Adapted, F. R. H.)	1869	Unpublished MS.
247	Candia	11 11 11, 5.	W. H. Havergal.	1867	Unpublished MS.
231	Capernaum	98, 98	W. H. Havergal.	1860	
61	Carlisle	C. M.	From " Ravenscroft's Psalter." Harmonized by W. H. H.	1621	Old Church Psalmody.
69	Carmel	C. M.	W. H. Havergal	......	Hundred Tunes.
219	Carpus	888, 4	F. R. Havergal	1870	
170	Casiphia	84, 84, 8884	W. H. Havergal	1868	Unpublished MS.
190	Cassel	87, 87, 77......	Ancient German Choral. Harmonized by W. H. H.	....	Old Church Psalmody.
216	Chaldea.............	888............	W. H. Havergal. (Adapted, F. R. H.)	c1835	Unpublished MS.
214	Chapel Royal	886 D.	Dr. Boyce. Harmonized by W. H. H.	1745	Old Church Psalmody.
35	Chesalon	C. M.	W. H. Havergal	1854	Hundred Tunes.
70	Chester; or, "*A Prayer for the Queen's most excellent Majestie.*"	C. M.	From " Este's Psalter." Harmonized by W. H. H.	1590	Old Church Psalmody.
145	Chios	77, 77	W. H. Havergal	1859	Unpublished MS.
104	Claudia	65, 65	F. R. Havergal	1870	
196	Coburg	87, 87, 87; or 87, 87, 447	Ancient German Choral. Harmonized by W. H. H.	......	Old Church Psalmody.
234	Conway	10 10, 10 10 ..	Henry Lawes. Harmonized by W. H. H.	1637	Old Church Psalmody.
3	Crasselius; or, *Winchester New*	L. M.	Crasselius, a Lutheran Presbyter at Düsseldorf. Harmonized by W. H. H.	c1650	Old Church Psalmody.
244	Crescens	11 8, 11 8	F. R. Havergal	1870	
22	Crete	L. M.	W. H. Havergal	1859	" Year of Praise," &c.
181	Culbach.............	87, 87	From Töpler's " Alte Choral Melodien." Harmonized by W. H. H.	......	Old Church Psalmody.
71	Culross	C. M.	From the " Scotch Psalter." Harmonized by W. H. H.	1635	Old Church Psalmody.
26	Cyprus	L. M.	W. H. Havergal	1861	Unpublished MS.
92	Cyrene	S. M.	W. H. Havergal	1860	Unpublished MS.
20	Dalmatia	L. M.	W. H. Havergal	1859	
111	Damaris	66, 66	F. R. Havergal............	1870	
218	Dies Iræ	888............	F. R. Havergal	1870	
64	Dimon	C. M.	W. H. Havergal. Composed in a dream	1853	Hundred Tunes.
21	Dortmund............	L. M.	From the " Hamburg Choral Book." Harmonized by W. H. H.	......	Old Church Psalmody
72	Dundee; or, *Windsor*	C. M.	From the " Scotch Psalter." Harmonized by W. H. H.	1615	Old Church Psalmody.
68	Dunfermline	C. M.	From " Ravenscroft's Psalter." Harmonized by W. H. H.	1621	Old Church Psalmody.
236	Ebronah	10 10, 10 10 ...	W. H. Havergal	1867	Unpublished MS.
38	Eden	C. M.	W. H. Havergal............	1845	Hundred Tunes.

Index of Tunes.   [229]   iii

No.	Name.	Measure.	Author or Harmonist.	Date.	Source.
246	Eirene	11 10, 11 10 ; or, 11 10, 11 10, 10 10	F. R. Havergal	1870	
252	"Ein' feste Burg"	8 7, 8 7, 6666, 7	Martin Luther	1529	
34	Elah	C. M.	W. H. Havergal	1845	Hundred Tunes.
124	Enon	6 7, 8 7	F. R. Havergal	1870	
II.	Ephesus	Hymn Chant	W. H. Havergal	1836	Hundred Chants.
57	Ephron	C. M.	W. H. Havergal	1838	Hundred Tunes.
6	Eppendorf	L. M.	C. P. Emmanuel Bach. Harmonized by W. H. H.	Ob. 1778	Old Church Psalmody.
8	Erfurt	L. M.	Dr. Martin Luther. From " Winterfeld's Collection of his Tunes. Leipsic, 1840." Harmonized by W. H. H.	1523	Old Church Psalmody
202	Esdraelon	8 7, 8 7 D.	W. H. Havergal. Arranged by F. R. H.	c 1838	From a Sacred Song.
221	Eshcol	8 8 8, 6	W. H. Havergal. (Adapted, F. R. H.)	1852	Hundred Tunes.
2	Euphrates	L. M.	W. H. Havergal	1848	Hundred Tunes.
54	Evan I.	C. M.	W. H. Havergal	1846	Cantica Laudis, Boston, U.S., &c.
77	Evan II.	C. M. D.	W. H. Havergal	1846	Unpublished MS.
230	Exeter	8 8 8 D.	From Hugh Bond's (of Exeter) "Selection of Psalm Tunes." Harmonized by W. H. H.	c 1795	Old Church Psalmody.
67	Farrant	C. M.	Richard Farrant, Gentleman of the Chapel Royal. Harmonized by W. H. H.	Ob. 1585	Old Church Psalmody.
87	Franconia	S. M.	German Melody. Harmonized by W. H. H.	c 1720	Old Church Psalmody
183	Frankfort	8 7, 8 7	G. Joseph, of Breslau	1690	Old Church Psalmody.
65	French ; or, *Dundee*	C. M.	From the "Scotch Psalter." Harmonized by W. H. H.	1615	Old Church Psalmody.
25	Galilee	L. M.	W. H. Havergal	1867	Unpublished MS.
131	Gareb	7 6, 7 6, 7 7, 7 6	W. H. Havergal	1848	" Liverpool Tunebook," &c., &c.
233	Gedor	10 10, 7	W. H. Havergal	1867	Unpublished MS.
17	Gennesaret	L. M.	W. H. Havergal	1844	Hundred Tunes.
10	Gerar	L. M.	W. H. Havergal	1856	Hundred Tunes.
28	Gethsemane	L. M.	W. H. Havergal	1838	Hundred Tunes.
148	Gibbons	7 7, 7 7	Orlando Gibbons. Harmonized by W. H. H.	1623	Old Church Psalmody.
11	Gilboa	L. M.	W. H. Havergal	1849	Hundred Tunes.
40	Gloucester	C. M.	From " Ravenscroft's Psalter." Harmonized by W. H. H.	1621	Old Church Psalmody.
185	Godesberg	8 7, 8 7	From the "Arien" of H. Albert. Harmonized by W. H. H.	1644	Old Church Psalmody.
130	Goldbach	7 6, 7 6; or, 7 6, 7 6 D.	Vulpius and C. P. E. Bach. From the "Hamburg Choral Book." Harmonized by W. H. H.	......	Old Church Psalmody
7	Göldel	L. M.	German Choral. The usual words to it by John Göldel, Presbyter. Died at Dienstadt, 1685. Harmonized by W. H. H.	Before 1627	Old Church Psalmody.
115	Gopsal	6 6 6 6, 4 4 4 4	Handel. From the Fitzwilliam MSS. Arranged by W. H. H.	c 1742	Old Church Psalmody.

iv   *Index of Tunes.*   [230]

No.	Name.	Measure.	Author or Harmonist.	Date.	Source.
125	Goshen	76, 76	W. H. Havergal	1863	"Fireside Music."
165	Gozan	77, 87	W. H. Havergal. (Adapted, F. R. H.)	1849	Hundred Tunes.
205	Hamburg	87, 87 D.	John Schoppe. Harmonized by W. H. H.	1642	Old Church Psalmody.
239	Hanover ; or, Croft's 104th	10 10, 11 11	From Supplement to N. V. Dr. Croft. Harmonized by W. H. H.	1708	Old Church Psalmody
9	Haran ; or, Bertram	L. M.	W. H. Havergal	......	"Anglican Hymn book," &c.
30	Hareth	L. M.	W. H. Havergal	......	Hundred Tunes.
133	Havergal	777	} W. H. Havergal {	Ap 16 1870	} Unpublished MS.
163	Havergal	777, 777, 777			
192	Havilah	87, 87, 87	W. H. Havergal	1870	Unpublished MS.
12	Hebron	L. M.	W. H. Havergal	1852	Hundred Tunes.
105	Hermas	65, 65 D.	F. R. Havergal	1870	
27	Hermon	L. M.	W. H. Havergal	1840	Hundred Tunes.
160	Heshbon ; or, Parracombe	77, 77 D.	W. H. Havergal	1869	Rev. L. C. Biggs' "Supplement to Hymns Ancient and Modern."
31	Hiddekel	L. M.	W. H. Havergal	......	Hundred Tunes.
248	Hobah	11 11, 11 11	W. H. Havergal	1846	
16	Hor	L. M.	W. H. Havergal	......	Hundred Tunes.
193	Idumea	87, 87, 87	W. H. Havergal. (Adapted, F. R. H.)	1866	Unpublished MS.
37	Iona	C. M.	W. H. Havergal	1869	Unpublished MS.
91	Jeruel ; or, Hawkstone	S. M.	W. H. Havergal	1869	Unpublished MS.
220	Jezreel	888, 6.	W. H. Havergal	......	Hundred Tunes.
211	Jordan	886 D.	W. H. Havergal	1851	Hundred Tunes.
140	Judea	77, 77	W. H. Havergal	1854	Unpublished MS.
159	Kadesh	7777 D; or, 10 lines, 7 s	W. H. Havergal	1869	Unpublished MS.
42	Kedar	C. M.	W. H. Havergal	1859	Unpublished MS.
213	Kedron	886 D.	W. H. Havergal	......	Hundred Tunes.
63	Kent	C. M.	Supposed old English tune used in Kent. Harmonized by W. H. H.	......	Old Church Psalmody
132	Kiriathaim	76, 86, 86, 86	W. H. Havergal	1869	Unpublished MS.
VIII.	Laodicea	Hymn Chant	F. R. Havergal	1870	
177	Lebanon	86, 86, 88	W. H. Havergal	......	Hundred Tunes.
19	Leipsic	L. M.	John Hermann Schein, Music Director. Died at Leipsic, 1631. Harmonized by W. H. H.	......	Old Church Psalmody.
55	London New ; or, Newton	C. M.	From the "Scotch Psalter." Harmonized by W. H. H.	1635	Old Church Psalmody.
139	Lubeck	77, 77	Ancient German Choral. Harmonized by W. H. H.	......	Old Church Psalmody.
95	Ludlow	S. M.	From "Ravenscroft's Psalter." Harmonized by W. H. H.	1621	Old Church Psalmody.
199	Lusatia	87, 87, 447	German Choral. Harmonized by W. H. H.	......	Old Church Psalmody.

Index of Tunes.   [23]   v

No.	Name.	Measure.	Author or Harmonist.	Date.	Source.
152	Luxemburg	7 7, 7 7	Ancient German Choral. Harmonized by W. H. H.	......	Old Church Psalmody.
210	Magdalene College	8 8 6 D.	Dr. W. Hayes. Harmonized by W. H. H.	1780	Old Church Psalmody.
129	Mahanaim............	7 6, 7 6 D.	W. H. Havergal	Jan. 1870	Unpublished MS.
226	Mamre	8 8, 8 8, 8 8 ; or, 9 8, 9 8, 8 8...	W. H. Havergal	......	Hundred Tunes.
229	Maon..................	8 8, 8 8, 8 8 ...	W. H. Havergal	......	Hundred Tunes.
154	Marah	7 7, 7 7	W. H. Havergal	1861	Unpublished MS.
93	Marano	S. M.	From "La Scala Santa." Harmonized by W. H. H.	1681	Old Church Psalmody.
96	Massah	S. M. D.	W. H. Havergal	......	Hundred Tunes.
195	Media	8 7, 8 7, 8 7......	W. H. Havergal	1859	Unpublished MS.
122	Megiddon	6 6, 8 6, 8 8......	W. H. Havergal. (Adapted, F. R. H.)	......	Hundred Tunes.
24	Melcombe............	L. M.	S. Webbe. Harmonized by W. H. H.	1812	Old Church Psalmody.
50	Melross	C. M..............	From the "Scotch Psalter." Harmonized by W. H. H.	1635	Old Church Psalmody.
228	Meribah	8 8, 8 8, 8 8......	W. H. Havergal	......	Hundred Tunes.
215	Merom	8 8 7, 8 8 7......	W. H. Havergal. (Adapted, F. R. H.)	......	Hundred Tunes.
175	Midian	8 6, 8 6, 4	W. H. Havergal. (Adapted, F. R. H.)	1861	Unpublished MS.
126	Minden	7 6, 7 6, 7 7......	From Töpler's "Alte Choral Melodien." Harmonized by W. H. H.	......	Old Church Psalmody.
120	Mizpeh	6 6 6 6, 8 8.	W. H. Havergal	1851	Hundred Tunes.
83	Moravia...............	S. M...............	Rev. Lewis West. Harmonized by W. H. H.	c1800	Old Church Psalmody.
119	Moriah	6 6 6 6, 8 8.......	W. H. Havergal	1846	Hundred Tunes.
107	Moscow	6 6 4, 6 6 6 4	Attributed, in the "Lock Collection," to Giardini. Harmonized by W. H. H............................	c1760	Old Church Psalmody.
80	Narenza	S. M.	Ancient Choral, from the "Cologne Hymn Book." Harmonized by W. H. H.	......	Old Church Psalmody.
155	Nassau	7 7, 7 7, 7 7......	John Rosenmüller, Director of Music at Leipsic. Harmonized by W. H. H.	1655	Old Church Psalmody.
47	Nayland ; or, *St. Stephen*	C. M.	Rev. W. Jones, of Nayland. Harmonized by W. H. H.	c1780	Common Praise.
121	Nebo	6 6 6 6, 8 8.......	W. H. Havergal	1848	Hundred Tunes.
212	New College.........	8 8 6 D.	Dr. W. Hayes. Harmonized by W. H. H.	1780	Old Church Psalmody.
100	Nimrim...............	6 4, 6 4, 6 6 4....	W. H. Havergal	1857	Hundred Tunes.
39	Nottingham ; or, *St. Magnus*	C. M.	Jeremiah Clark. Harmonized by W. H. H.	1700	Old Church Psalmody.
251	"Nun danket alle Gott"............ ...	6 7, 6 7, 6 6 6 6.	Johann Crüger	1649	
97	Old 25th	S. M. D...........	From "Day's Psalter." Harmonized by W. H. H.	1563	Old Church Psalmody.
74	Old 44th	C. M. D..., ..	From "Day's Psalter." Harmonized by W. H. H.	1563	Old Church Psalmody.
75	Old 81st...............	C. M. D...........	From "Day's Psalter"...............	1563	Old Church Psalmody.
1	Old 100th*	L. M.	Melody from "Day's Psalter." Harmonized by W. H. H.	1563	Old Church Psalmody.
	Another of the same	L. M.	From the "Psalter." Harmonized by W. H. H.	1580	Old Church Psalmody.

* See "A History of the Old Hundredth," by the Rev. W. H. Havergal.

vi   *Index of Tunes.*   [232]

No.	Name.	Measure.	Author or Harmonist.	Date.	Source.
237	Old 124th	10 10 10, 10 10	From ' Day's Psalter." Harmonized by W. H. H.	1563	Old Church Psalmody.
78	Old Nunc Dimittis	C. M. D.	In all the old Psalters. Harmonized by W. H. H.	......	Old Church Psalmody.
15	Old Ten Commandments; or, *Commandments*	L. M.	From the "Genevan Psalter." Harmonized by W. H. H.	1562	Old Church Psalmody.
146	Oldenburg	7 7, 7 7	Ancient German Choral	......	Old Church Psalmody.
101	Olivet	6 4, 6 4, 6 6 4	W. H. Havergal	1857	Hundred Tunes.
109	Ono	6 6 4, 6 6 6 4	W. H. Havergal	c1825	Hundred Tunes.
235	Ophir	10 10, 10 10	W. H. Havergal	1867	Unpublished MS.
108	Oreb	6 6 4, 6 6 6 4	W. H. Havergal	......	Hundred Tunes.
241	Paran	10 10, 11 11 ; or, 11 11, 11 11	W. H. Havergal	c1857	Hundred Tunes.
147	Patmos	7 7, 7 7	W. H. Havergal	1869	Unpublished MS.
23	Peniel	L. M.	W. H. Havergal	1867	Unpublished MS.
242	Peor	11 11, 10 10; or, 11 11, 11 11	W. H. Havergal	......	Hundred Tunes.
143	Perazim	7 7, 7 7	W. H. Havergal	......	Hundred Tunes.
IV.	Pergamos	Hymn Chant.	F. R. Havergal	1870	
187	Persis	8 7, 8 7, 3	F. R. Havergal	1870	
156	Pharpar	7 7, 7 7, 7 7	W. H. Havergal. (Adapted, F. R. H.)	......	Unpublished MS.
VII.	Philadelphia	Hymn Chant	F. R. Havergal	1870	
223	Philemon	8 8 8, 7	F. R. Havergal	1870	
137	Pisgah	7 7, 7 7	W. H. Havergal	1838	Hundred Tunes.
144	Pison	7 7, 7 7	W. H. Havergal	......	Hundred Tunes.
171	Prague	8 5, 8 5 ; or, 8 5, 8 3	German Choral. Harmonized by W. H. H. (Adapted, F. R. H.)	......	Old Church Psalmody.
114	Psalm 148th, O.V.	6 6 6 6, 4 4 4 4	Dr. Croft. Harmonized by W. H. H.	......	Old Church Psalmody.
113	Psalm 148th, N.V.	6 6 6 6, 4 4 4 4	Dr. Howard. Harmonized by W. H. H.	1770	Old Church Psalmody.
134	Ramah	7 7 7	W. H. Havergal. (Adapted, F. R. H.)	1861	Unpublished MS.
157	Ratisbon	7 7, 7 7, 7 7	From Werner's "New Saxon Choral Book." Harmonized by W. H. H.	1815	Old Church Psalmody.
141	Rephaim	7 7, 7 7	W. H. Havergal	......	Hundred Tunes.
150	Rimmon	7 7, 7 7	W. H. Havergal	......	Hundred Tunes.
240	Ripon	10 10, 11 11	John Church, Gentleman of the Chapel Royal. Harmonized by W. H. H.	1698	Old Church Psalmody.
33	Rostoc	L. M. D.	German Choral. Harmonized by W. H. H.	......	Old Church Psalmody.
62	Salisbury	C. M.	From Ravenscroft's Psalter. Harmonized by W. H. H.	1621	Old Church Psalmody.
167	Salmon	7 8, 7 8	W. H. Havergal. (Adapted, F. R. H.)	1842	Hundred Tunes.
203	Salzburg	8 7, 8 7 D.	Michael Haydn. Harmonized by W. H. H.	1700	Old Church Psalmody.
162	Samaria	7 7, 7 7 D.	W. H. Havergal. (Adapted, F. R. H.)	......	Hundred Tunes.
135	Samos	7 7 7, 3	W. H. Havergal. (Adapted, F. R. H.)	1859	Unpublished MS.
VI.	Sardis	Hymn Chant	F. R. Havergal	1870	
32	Saxony	L. M.	Ancient German Choral. Harmonized by W. H. H.	Before 1588	Old Church Psalmody

Index of Tunes.   [233]   vi

No.	Name.	Measure.	Author or Harmonist.	Date.	Source.
161	Seir	7 7, 7 7 D.	W. H. Havergal	1850	Hundred Tunes.
14	Selnecker	L. M.	Dr. Nicholas Selnecker, Professor of Theology at Leipsic. Harmonized by W. H. H.	Ob. 1592	Old Church Psalmody
142	Sephar	7 7, 7 7	W. H. Havergal	1854	Hundred Tunes.
117	Sheba	6 6 6 6 D.	W. H. Havergal. (Adapted, F. R. H.)	1865	Unpublished MS.
201	Shen	8 7, 8 7 D.	W. H. Havergal. (Adapted, F. R. H.)	1853	Hundred Tunes.
136	Shenir I.	7 7 7, 5	W. H. Havergal. (Adapted, F. R. H.)	1850	Hundred Tunes.
151	Shenir II.	7 7, 7 7	W. H. Havergal	1850	Hundred Tunes.
204	Shinar	8 7, 8 7 D.	W. H. Havergal. (Adapted, F. R. H.)	1865	Unpublished MS.
158	Sihor	7 7, 7 7, 7 7	W. H. Havergal. (Adapted, F. R. H.)	1851	Hundred Tunes.
153	Siloam	7 7, 7 7	W. H. Havergal	......	Hundred Tunes.
176	Silvanus	8 6, 8 6, 8 6	F. R. Havergal	1870	
178	Sirah	8 7, 8 7	W. H. Havergal	c 1826	Hundred Tunes.
180	Sirion	8 7, 8 7	W. H. Havergal	1851	Hundred Tunes.
179	Sitnah	8 7, 8 7	W. H. Havergal	1842	Hundred Tunes.
III.	Smyrna	Hymn Chant	W. H. Havergal	1836	Hundred Chants.
184	Sorek	8 7, 8 7	W. H. Havergal	......	Hundred Tunes.
243	Sosthenes	10 11, 11 11, 12 11	F. R. Havergal	1870	
94	Southwell	S. M.	From the Psalter printed by Henrie Denham. Harmonized by W. H. H.	1588	Old Church Psalmody.
29	Spires	L. M.	From the Psalter. Harmonized by W. H. H.	1563	Old Church Psalmody.
52	St. Ann	C. M.	Denby. Abraham Barber's "Book of Psalm Tunes." Harmonized by W. H. H.	1686	Old Church Psalmody.
106	St. Barnabas	6 5, 6 5 D.	F. R. Havergal	1870	
95a	St. Bride	S. M.	Dr. Howard. Harmonized by W. H. H.	c 1770	Old Church Psalmody.
53	St. Chrysostom	C. M.	W. H. Havergal	c 1830	Unpublished MS.
60	St. David	C. M.	From Playford's Psalter. Harmonized by W. H. H.	1671	Old Church Psalmody.
49	St. James	C. M.	Raphael Courteville, Gentleman of the Chapel Royal. Harmonized by W. H. H.	1680	Old Church Psalmody.
73	St. Mary; or, *Hackney*	C. M.	From Playford's Psalter. Harmonized by W. H. H.	1671	Old Church Psalmody and Common Praise
58	St. Matthias	C. M.	Orlando Gibbons. Harmonized by W. H. H.	1623	Old Church Psalmody
85	St. Michael	S. M.	From the Psalter of 1565, and from that "printed for the assignees of R. Day, 1588." Harmonized by W. H. H.	1565	Old Church Psalmody
253	St. Paul	8 7, 8 8 7, 7 7, 7 7	F. R. Havergal	1871	
98	St. Silas	5 5 5 5, 6 5 6 5	F. R. Havergal	1870	
168	Stephanas	8 3, 8 3, 8 8 8, 3 3	F. R. Havergal	1870	
245	Sternberg	11 10, 11 10	From Freylinghausen's Gesangbuch	1704	Old Church Psalmody
110	Stobel	6 6 4, 6 6 6 4	From J. D. Müller's "Choral Buch." Harmonized by W. H. H.	1754	Old Church Psalmody
182	Stuttgard	8 7, 8 7	German Choral. Harmonized by W. H. H.	......	Old Church Psalmody

No.	Name.	Measure.	Author or Harmonist.	Date.	Source.
189	Succoth	8 7, 8 7, 7 7	W. H. Havergal. (Adapted, F. R. H.)	......	Hundred Tunes.
82	Swabia	S. M.	Ancient German Melody. Harmonized by W. H. H.	......	Old Church Psalmody.
197	Tabor	8 7, 8 7, 8 7; or, 8 7, 8 7, 4 4 7	W. H. Havergal	......	Hundred Tunes.
13	Tallis's Canon	L. M.	Abridged by Ravenscroft, 1621, from Archbp. Parker's Psalter, 1561. Harmonized by W. H. H.	1561	Old Church Psalmody.
44	Tallis; or, *Tallis's Ordinal*	C. M.	Thomas Tallis (originally Talys). From Archbp. Parker's Psalter	c 1561	Old Church Psalmody.
200	Tekoa	8 7, 8 7, 8 7; or, 8 7, 8 7, 4 4 7	W. H. Havergal	1852	Hundred Tunes.
194	Teman	8 7, 8 7, 8 7	W. H. Havergal	1869	Unpublished MS.
V.	Thyatira	Hymn Chant	F. R. Havergal	1870	
169	Tiberias	8 4, 8 4, 8 8 8 4	W. H. Havergal	1869	Unpublished MS.
249	Trisagion	11 12, 12 10	W. H. Havergal	1850	
123	Trophimus	6 6 9	F. R. Havergal	1870	
217	Tryphena	8 8 8	F. R. Havergal	1870	
209	Tryphosa	8 8 6	F. R. Havergal	1870	
198	Ulai	8 7, 8 7, 8 7; or, 4 4 7	W. H. Havergal	......	Hundred Tunes.
250	Venite Adoremus	12 10, 11 10	W. H. Havergal	1866	Unpublished MS.
149	Vienna	7 7, 7 7	German Choral. Harmonized by W. H. H.	......	Old Church Psalmody.
4	Waldeck	L. M.	Ancient German Choral. Harmonized by W. H. H.	......	Old Church Psalmody.
5	Wells	L. M.	Genevan Choral. Harmonized by W. H. H.	......	Unpublished MS.
46	Winchester	C. M.	From Alison's Psalter	1599	Old Church Psalmody.
I.	Worcester	Hymn Chant	W. H. Havergal	1836	Hundred Chants.
45	York	C. M.	From the Scotch Psalter	1615	Old Church Psalmody.
191	Zaanaim	8 7, 8 7, 8 7; or, 4 4 7	W. H. Havergal	1849	Hundred Tunes.
172	Zared I.	8 5, 8 5, 7 7 7, 5	W. H. Havergal	1849	"Hymn for Christmas Day," 1849.
173	Zared II.	8 5, 8 5, 8 4 3	Arranged by W. H. H. from Zared I.	1868	Unpublished MS.
128	Zeboim	7 6, 7 6 D.	W. H. Havergal	c 1858	Hundred Tunes.
238	Zemaraim	10 10, 10 10, 10 10	W. H. Havergal	1867	Unpublished MS.
127	Zoan I.	7 6, 7 6 D.	W. H. Havergal	1845	Hundred Tunes.
166	Zoan II.	7 7, 8 7 D.	W. H. Havergal. (Adapted, F. R. H.)	......	
207	Zoheleth	8 7, 8 7, 8 8 7	W. H. Havergal	c 1858	Hundred Tunes.
99	Zophim	5 5, 7 7 7 7, 6	W. H. Havergal	......	Hundred Tunes.

ix   [235]

II.

INDEX OF SUITABLE WORDS.

(ALPHABETICALLY ARRANGED).

Words.	No.	Tune.	Words.	No.	Tune.
Abide with me {	235	Ophir, or	Come see the place	210 {	Magdalene
	236	Ebronah			College
Accepted, perfect and complete	217	Tryphena	Come, Thou Fount	202	Esdraelon
All hail, adorèd Trinity	7	Göldel	Come to Thy temple, Lord	84	Amana
All hail the power of Jesu's	34	Elah	Come, ye thankful people, come	160	Heshbon
All people that on earth	1	Old Hundredth	Come, ye that love the Lord	81	Abana
Almighty Lord, before Thy	73	St. Mary	Conquering kings their titles	143	Perazim
And will the Judge descend	93	Marano	Creator Spirit, by whose aid	227	Angels' Song
Angels from the realms of glory	193	Idumea			
Angel voices ever singing	173	Zared II.	Day of judgment, day of wonders	197	Tabor
A pilgrim through this lonely	71	Culross	Day of wrath, O day of mourning	218	Dies Iræ
Art Thou, Lord, rebuking	200	Tekoa	Dread Jehovah	206	Augsburg
As pants the hart	48	Adria			
Awake, and sing the song	79	Aven	Earth below is teeming	105	Hermas
Awake, my soul, in joyful lays	6	Eppendorf	Eternity, eternity	29	Spires
Before Jehovah's awful throne	1	Old Hundredth	Far from my heavenly home	95	Ludlow
Before the Almighty power	33	Rostoc	Father, I know that all my life	176	Silvanus
Begin, my tongue,	40	Gloucester	Father of heaven, whose love	18	Bavaria
Behold the Lamb of God	118	Arnon	Father of mercies, in Thy word	50	Melross
Behold the mountain of the Lord	45	York	Father, whose hand	246	Eirene
Behold the throne of grace	87	Franconia	For mercies countless	61	Carlisle
Behold what wondrous grace	92	Cyrene	From Greenland's icy mountains	127	Zoan I.
Blow ye the trumpet, blow	115	Gopsal	From whence this fear	214	Chapel Royal
Bound upon the accursèd tree	164	Calvary			
Bread of the world	231	Capernaum	Give me the wings of faith	46	Winchester
Breast the wave, Christian	98	St. Silas	Glorious things of thee	203	Salzburg
Brethren, let us join to bless	146	Oldenburg	Glory, glory everlasting	191	Zaanaim
Brighter than meridian	192	Havilah	Glory, glory to our King	156	Pharpar
Brightest and best of the sons	245	Sternberg	Glory to God on high	108	Oreb
Bring to Christ your best	223	Philemon	Glory to Thee, my God	13	Tallis's Canon
By angels in heaven	239	Hanover	God is the refuge of His saints	15	Old Ten Commandments.
Captain of Thine enlisted host	11	Gilboa	God moves in a mysterious way	60	St David
Children of the heavenly King	149	Vienna	God of my life; to Thee I call	31	Hiddekel
Christian, seek not yet repose	135	Samos	God that madest earth	170	Casiphia
Christians, awake! salute	238	Zemaraim	Great God, what do I see	208	Altorf
Christ is our corner stone	113	Ps. 148th, N.V.	Guide me, O Thou great	195	Media
Christ the Lord is risen again	141	Rephaim			
Christ the Lord is risen to-day	138	Abilene	Hail, Thou once despised	204	Shinar
Christ whose glory fills the skies	157	Ratisbon	Hallelujah, Hallelujah! Hearts	201	Shen
Come, gracious Spirit	20	Dalmatia	Hallelujah, Lord, our voices	182	Stuttgart
Come, Holy Ghost {	21	Dortmund, or	Happy Christian, God's own	148	Gibbons
	22	Crete	Hark, my soul, it is the Lord	151	Shenir II.
Come, Holy Spirit, come	90	Armageddon	Hark! ten thousand voices	180	Sirion
Come, Holy Spirit, heavenly	44	Tallis	Hark! the glad sound	43	Bristol
Come, labour on! {	Hymn Chant VII. }	} Philadelphia	Hark! the song of jubilee	137	Pisgah
			Hark! what mean those holy	179	Sitnah
			Have mercy, Lord, on me	95a	St. Bride
Come let us join our cheerful	38	Eden	Head of Thy Church	166	Zoan II.
Come, oh come, in pious lays	159	Kadesh	He came, whose embassy was	74	Old 44th

Words.	No.	Tune.	Words.	No.	Tune.
Holy Ghost, my Comforter	134	Ramah	Lord, as to Thy dear cross	69	Carmel
Holy, holy, holy ! Lord God	249	Trisagion	Lord, I hear of showers	187	Persis
Holy Spirit, from on high	152	Luxemburg	Lord of mercy and of might	136	Shenir I
Hope, Christian soul	219	Carpus	Lord of our Life	247	Candia
Hosanna, raise the pealing hymn	35	Chesalon	Lord of the worlds above	114	Ps. 148th, o.v
Hosanna to the living Lord	225	Baden II.	Lord, Thy word abideth	111	Damaris
How sweet the name of Jesus	65	French	Lord, when before Thy throne	177	Lebanon
			Lord, when we bend	70	Chester
I gave my life for thee	116	Baca	Love, only Love	212	New College
I heard the voice of Jesus	77	Evan II.	Loving Shepherd	145	Chios
I journey through a desert drear	236	Ebronah			
I know that my Redeemer	12	Hebron	Mighty Father, blessed Son	163	Havergal
I lay my sins on Jesus	129	Mahanaim	My faith looks up to Thee	110	Stobel
I'm but a stranger here	102	Beulah	My God, my Father	220	Jezreel
Incarnate God, the soul	62	Salisbury	My God, the covenant	42	Kedar
I need no other plea	122	Megiddon	My heart is fixed, eternal God	168	Stephanas
In songs of sublime adoration	244	Crescens	Nearer, my God, to Thee {	100	Nimrim
In sorrow and distress	94	Southwell		101	Olivet
Inspirer and Hearer of prayer	224	Aristarchus	New every morning is the love	16	Hor
In the hour of trial	106	St. Barnabas	Not all the blood of beasts	86	Ajalon
In the sun and moon and stars	153	Siloam	Now gracious Lord	52	St. Ann
In Thy glorious Resurrection	215	Merom	Now thank we all our God	251 {	"Nun danke alle Gott"
Isles of the deep, rejoice	37	Iona	O come, all ye faithful	250 {	Venite Adoremus
Israel's Shepherd, guide me,	183	Frankfort			
I thought upon my sins { Hymn Chant VI.		Sardis	O day of rest and gladness	130	Goldbach
			O faint and feeble-hearted	125	Goshen
I was a wandering sheep	88	Achor	O God of Hosts { Hymn Chant I.		Worcester
I will go in the strength	232	Aquila			
Jehovah Elohim, Creator great	234	Conway	O God, our help in ages past { 55 Hymn Chant III.		LondonNew or, Smyrna
Jerusalem, Jerusalem	75	Old 81st			
Jerusalem, my happy home	47	Nayland			
Jesus calls us, o'er the tumult	185	Godesberg	O help us, Lord	72	Dundee
Jesus Christ is risen to-day	140	Judea	O holy Saviour, Friend unseen	221	Eshcol
Jesus from the skies descending	172	Zared I.	O King of Kings, Thy blessing	14	Selneckcr
Jesus, I my cross have taken	205	Hamburg	O Love divine, how sweet	213	Kedron
Jesus lives ! no longer now	167	Salmon	O praise the Lord in that	10	Gerar
Jesu, Lover of my soul	161	Seir	O render thanks to God above	4	Waldeck
Jesu, meek and gentle	104	Claudia	O sons and daughters, let us sing	216	Chaldea
Jesus shall reign where'er the	8	Erfurt	O Spirit of the living God	9	Haran
Jesus, Sun and Shield art Thou	126	Minden	O Thou from whom all goodness	68	Dunfermline
Jesus, the very thought of Thee	54	Evan I.	O worship the King	241	Paran
Jesus, Thou joy of loving hearts	26	Cyprus	Oft in danger, oft in woe	144	Pison
Jesus, Thy blood	28	Gethsemane	Oh ! for a burst of praise to God	230	Exeter
Jesus, to Thy table led	133	Havergal	Oh ! for a heart to praise my God	66	Bedford
Join all the glorious names	121	Nebo	Oh ! what a lonely path	59	Arran
Just as I am, without one plea {	25	Galilee, or	One sweetly solemn thought { Hymn Chant V.		Thyatira
	222	Bethabara I.			
Just as Thou art	222	Bethabara II.	One there is above all others	189	Succoth
Lay the precious body	106	St. Barnabas	Onward, holy champion	105	Hermas
Lead us, heavenly Father,	199	Lusatia	Our blest Redeemer	174	Bethany
Let me be with Thee	17	Gennesaret	Our God is love	58	St. Matthias
Let us with a gladsome mind	139	Lubeck	Our year of grace	237	Old 124th
Let Zion in her songs record	211	Jordan			
Lo ! He comes	196	Coburg	Plunged in a gulph	56	Caithness
Long did I toil { Hymn Chant VIII.		Laodicea	Praise the Lord, ye heavens	181	Culbach

xii   No. III.—METRICAL INDEX.   [238]

For irregular measures of four lines, see Hymn Chants, Nos. IV., V., and VI. ; Do. five lines, No. VII. Do. six lines, No. VIII

xiii   [239]

IV.

NUMERICAL INDEX.

No.	Name.	Suitable Words.	No.	Name.	Suitable Words.
	L. M.		47	Nayland	Jerusalem, my happy home.
1	Old Hundredth ...	All people that on earth.	48	Adria	As pants the hart for cooling.
	Another of the same	Before Jehovah's awful throne.	49	St. James	Thou art the Way.
2	Euphrates	What are those soul-reviving.	50	Melross	Father of mercies, in Thy word.
3	Crasselius	The Saviour lives.	51	Besor	What shall I render to my God?
4	Waldeck	O render thanks to God.	52	St. Ann	Now, gracious Lord.
5	Wells	Soon may the last glad song.	53	St. Chrysostom ...	Wake, harp of Zion.
6	Eppendorf	Awake, my soul.	54	Evan I.	Jesus, the very thought of Thee.
7	Göldel	All hail, adorèd Trinity.	55	London New	O God, our help in ages past.
8	Erfurt	Jesus shall reign.	56	Caithness	Plunged in a gulph.
9	Haran	O Spirit of the living God.	57	Ephron	When all Thy mercies.
10	Gerar	O praise the Lord.	58	St. Matthias	Our God is love.
11	Gilboa	Captain of Thine enlisted host.	59	Arran	Oh, what a lonely path.
12	Hebron	I know that my Redeemer.	60	St. David	God moves in a mysterious way.
13	Tallis's Canon ...	Glory to Thee, my God.	61	Carlisle	For mercies countless.
14	Selnecker	O King of kings.	62	Salisbury	Incarnate God.
15	Old Ten Commandments	God is the refuge.	63	Kent	When I can read my title clear.
			64	Dimon..............	Why should the children.
16	Hor	New every morning is the love.	65	French..............	How sweet the name of Jesus.
17	Gennesaret	Let me be with Thee.	66	Bedford	Through all the changing.
18	Bavaria	Father of heaven! whose love		Do. (Common time)	Oh, for a heart to praise.
19	Leipsic	Take up thy cross.	67	Farrant	The saints on earth.
20	Dalmatia	Come, gracious Spirit.	68	Dunfermline	O Thou from whom.
21	Dortmund	Come, Holy Ghost.	69	Carmel	Lord, as to Thy dear cross.
22	Crete	Come, Holy Ghost.	70	Chester	Lord, when we bend.
23	Peniel	Sun of my soul, thou Saviour.	71	Culross	A pilgrim through this lonely.
24	Melcombe	Where high the heavenly.	72	Dundee	O help us, Lord, each hour.
25	Galilee..............	Just as I am, without one plea	73	St. Mary	Almighty God, before Thy.
26	Cyprus..............	Jesus, Thou joy of loving hearts.		**C. M. D.**	
27	Hermon	When I survey the wondrous.	74	Old 44th	He came, whose embassy.
28	Gethsemane	Jesus, Thy blood.	75	Old 81st	Jerusalem, Jerusalem!
29	Spires	Eternity, eternity!	76	Bethaven............	The roseate hues of early dawn.
30	Hareth..............	The Lord shall come!	77	Evan II.	I heard the voice of Jesus say.
31	Hiddekel............	God of my life! to Thee I call.	78	Old Nunc Dimittis	See what unbounded zeal.
32	Saxony	That day of wrath.		**S. M.**	
	L. M. D.		79	Aven	Awake, and sing the song.
33	Rostoc..............	Before the Almighty power.	80	Narenza	Stand up, and bless the Lord
	C. M.		81	Abana	Come ye that love the Lord.
34	Elah.................	All hail, the power of Jesu's.	82	Swabia	To God, the only wise.
35	Chesalon	Hosanna! raise the pealing.	83	Moravia	Ye servants of the Lord.
36	Bether	Salvation! O, the joyful sound.	84	Amana	Come to Thy temple, Lord.
37	Iona.................	Isles of the deep, rejoice.	85	St. Michael.........	To bless Thy chosen race.
38	Eden	Come, let us join our cheerful.	86	Ajalon..............	Not all the blood of beasts.
39	Nottingham	The Head that once.	87	Franconia	Behold the throne of grace.
40	Gloucester	Begin, my tongue.	88	Achor	I was a wandering sheep.
41	Berachah............	The Son of God goes forth.	89	Abarim	Sow in the morn thy seed.
42	Kedar	My God, the covenant.	90	Armageddon	Come, Holy Spirit, come.
43	Bristol	Hark, the glad sound.	91	uel	What cheering words are these?
44	Tallis	Come, Holy Spirit, heavenly.	92	Cyrene..............	Behold what wondrous grace.
45	York	Behold! the mountain	93	Marano	And will the Judge descend.
46	Winchester	Give me the wings of faith.			

No.	Name.	Suitable Words.
	S. M.	
94	Southwell	In sorrow and distress.
95	Ludlow	Far from my heavenly home.
95*a*	St. Bride	Have mercy, Lord, on me.
	S. M. D.	
96	Massah	Thou art gone up on high.
97	Old 25th	The Church has waited long.
	5555, 6565.	
98	St. Silas	Breast the wave, Christian.
	55, 7777, 6.	
99	Zophim	There was joy in heaven.
	64, 64, 664.	
100	Nimrim	Nearer, my God, to Thee.
101	Olivet	Nearer, my God, to Thee.
	64, 64, 6664.	
102	Beulah	I'm but a stranger here.
	64, 66.	
103	Amplias	The sun is sinking fast.
	65, 65.	
104	Claudia	Jesu, meek and gentle.
	65, 65 D.	
105	Hermas	{ Earth below is teeming, or Onward, holy champion.
106	St. Barnabas	{ Lay the precious body, or In the hour of trial.
	664, 6664.	
107	Moscow	Sound, sound the truth abroad.
108	Oreb	Glory to God on high.
109	Ono	Thou, whose Almighty word.
110	Stobel	My faith looks up to Thee.
	66, 66 Trochaic.	
111	Damaris	Lord, Thy word abideth.
	66, 66 Iambic.	
112	Bashan	Thy way, not mine, O Lord.
	6666, 4444.	
113	Psalm 148th, N. V.	Christ is our corner-stone.
114	Psalm 148th, O. V.	Lord of the worlds above.
115	Gopsal	Blow ye the trumpet, blow.
	6666, 66.	
116	Baca	I gave my life for thee.
	66, 66 D.	
117	Sheba	There is a blessèd home.
	66, 84.	
118	Arnon	Behold the Lamb of God.
	6666, 88.	
119	Moriah	Rejoice, the Lord is King.
120	Mizpeh	We give immortal praise.
121	Nebo	Join all the glorious names.
	66, 86, 88.	
122	Megiddon	I need no other plea.
	669.	
123	Trophimus	Spared a little longer.
	67, 87.	
124	Enon	Thou great mysterious Lord.
	76, 76.	
125	Goshen	{ O, faint and feeble hearted, or, Our faithful God.
	76, 76, 77.	
126	Minden	Jesus, Sun and Shield art Thou.
	76, 76 D.	
127	Zoan I.	From Greenland's icy.
	76, 76 D	
128	Zeboim	Sometimes a light surprises.
129	Mahanaim	I lay my sins on Jesus.
130	Goldbach	O day of rest and gladness.
	76, 76, 77, 76.	
131	Gareb	Rise, my soul, and stretch.
	76, 86, 86, 86.	
132	Kiriathaim	We won't give up the Bible.
	777.	
133	Havergal	Jesus, to Thy table led.
134	Ramah	Holy Ghost, my Comforter.
	777, 3.	
135	Samos	Christian, seek not yet repose
	777, 5.	
136	Shenir I.	Lord of mercy and of might.
	7777.	
137	Pisgah	Hark! the song of jubilee.
138	Abilene	Christ the Lord is risen to-day.
139	Lubeck	Let us with a gladsome mind.
140	Judea	Jesus Christ is risen to-day.
141	Rephaim	Christ the Lord is risen again.
142	Sephar	Sing, O heavens!
143	Perazim	Conquering kings their titles.
144	Pison	Oft in danger, oft in woe.
145	Chios	Loving Shepherd of Thy sheep.
146	Oldenburg	Brethren, let us join to bless.
147	Patmos	Thine for ever! God of love.
148	Gibbons	Happy Christian!
149	Vienna	Children of the heavenly King.
150	Rimmon	Softly now the light of day.
151	Shenir II.	Hark, my soul, it is the Lord.
152	Luxemburg	Holy Spirit, from on high.
153	Siloam	In the sun and moon.
154	Marah	See the destined day arise.
	77, 77, 77.	
155	Nassau	Sing, O sing this blessèd morn.
156	Pharpar	Glory, glory to our King.
157	Ratisbon	Christ, whose glory fills.
158	Sihor	Rock of ages, cleft for me.
	7777 D.	
159	Kadesh	Come, oh, come, in pious lays.
160	Heshbon	Come, ye thankful people.
161	Seir	Jesu, Lover of my soul.
162	Samaria	Who are these arrayed in white?
	777, 777, 777.	
163	Havergal	Mighty Father, blessèd Son.
	77, 77, 77, 77, 77.	
164	Calvary	Bound upon the accursèd tree.
	77, 87.	
165	Gozan	Thou God of grace, our Father.
	77, 87 D.	
166	Zoan II.	Head of Thy church.
	78, 78.	
167	Salmon	Jesus lives! no longer now.
	83, 83, 888, 33.	
168	Stephanas	My heart is fixed, eternal God
	84, 84, 8884.	
169	Tiberias	Through the love of God.
170	Casiphia	God, that madest earth.

Numerical Index.   〔241〕   XI

No.	Name.	Suitable Words.	No.	Name.	Suitable Words.
	85, 83, or 85, 85.		214	**886 D.** Chapel Royal	From whence this fear.
171	Prague	Thou who on that wondrous.		**887, 887.**	
	85, 85, 7775.		215	Merom	In Thy glorious resurrection.
172	Zared I.	Jesus, from the skies.		**888 Iambic.**	
	85, 85, 843.		216	Chaldea	O, sons and daughters.
173	Zared II.	Angel voices ever singing.	217	Tryphena	Accepted, perfect and complete.
	86, 84.			**888 Trochaic.**	
174	Bethany	Our blest Redeemer.	218	Dies Iræ	Day of wrath, O day.
	86, 86, 4.			**888, 4.**	
175	Midian	Return, O wanderer.	219	Carpus	Hope, Christian soul.
	86, 86, 86.		220	Jezreel	My God, my Father.
176	Silvanus	Father, I know that all my.		**888, 6.**	
	86, 86, 88.		221	Eshcol	O Holy Saviour.
177	Lebanon	Lord, when before Thy throne.	222	Bethabara	Just as I am, without one plea.
	87, 87.			Do. major	Just as Thou art.
178	Sirah	Soon the trumpet of salvation.		**888, 7.**	
179	Sitnah	Hark! what mean those holy.	223	Philemon	Bring to Christ your best.
180	Sirion	Hark! ten thousand voices.		**8888.**	
181	Culbach	Praise the Lord; ye heavens.	224	Aristarchus	Inspirer and hearer of prayer.
182	Stuttgard	Hallelujah! Lord, our voices.		**88, 88, 47.**	
183	Frankfort	Israel's Shepherd, guide me.	225	Baden II.	Hosanna to the living Lord.
184	Sorek	Sweet the moments.		**88, 88, 88.**	
185	Godesberg	Jesus calls us o'er the tumult.	226	Mamre	We sing His love.
186	Bremen	Shall this life of mine.	227	Angels' Song	Creator Spirit, by whose aid.
	87, 87, 3.		228	Meribah	Thou hidden love of God.
187	Persis	Lord, I hear of showers.	229	Maon	The Lord my pasture.
	87, 87, 44, 88.			**888, 888.**	
188	Baden I.	Whate'er my God ordains.	230	Exeter	Oh, for a burst of praise.
	87, 87, 77.			**9898.**	
189	Succoth	One there is above all others.	231	Capernaum	Bread of the world.
190	Cassel	Through the day Thy love.		**9998, 8888.**	
	8787, 87 (or 447)		232	Aquila	I will go in the strength.
191	Zaanaim	Glory, glory everlasting.		**1010, 7.**	
192	Havilah	Brighter than meridian.	233	Gedor	Sing Alleluia forth.
193	Idumea	Angels from the realms.		**1010, 1010.**	
194	Teman	To the name of our.	234	Conway	Jehovah Elohim, Creator great.
195	Media	Guide me, O Thou great.	235	Ophir	Abide with me.
196	Coburg	Lo, He comes with clouds.	236	Ebronah	{ I journey through a desert; or, Abide with me.
197	Tabor	Day of judgment.		**1010 1010, 1010.**	
198	Ulai	Widely midst the slumbering.	237	Old 124th	Our year of grace is wearing.
199	Lusatia	Lead us, heavenly Father.		**1010, 1010, 1010.**	
200	Tekoa	Art Thou, Lord, rebuking.	238	Zemaraim	Christians, awake!
	87, 87 D.			**1010, 1111.**	
201	Shen	Hallelujah, Hallelujah!	239	Hanover	By angels in heaven.
202	Esdraelon	Come, Thou Fount.	240	Ripon	Ye servants of God.
203	Salzburg	Glorious things of thee.		**1010, 1111, or 1111, 1111.**	
204	Shinar	Hail, Thou once despised.	241	Paran	O worship the King.
205	Hamburg	Jesus, I my cross have taken.	242	Peor	The night is far spent.
206	Augsburg	Dread Jehovah, God of nations		**1011, 1111, 1211.**	
	87, 87, 887.		243	Sosthenes	Sound the loud timbrel.
207	Zoheleth	The Lord of might.		**118, 118.**	
208	Altorf	Great God, what do I see?	244	Crescens	In songs of sublime adoration.
	886.			**1110, 1110.**	
209	Tryphosa	To Him who for our sins.	245	Sternberg	Brightest and best of the sons.
	886 D.			**1110, 1110 Iambic, or 1110, 1110, 1010.**	
210	Magdalene College	Come, see the place.	246	Eirene	{ Father whose hand hath led, or, Long did I toil.
211	Jordan	Let Zion in her songs record.			
212	New College	Love, only love, Thy heart.			
213	Kedron	O Love Divine, how sweet.			

No.	Name.	Suitable Words.	No.	Name.	Suitable Words.
247	**11 11 11, 5.** Candia..............	Lord of our life.	251	67, 67, 6666. "Nun danket" ...	Now thank we all our God.
248	**11 11, 11 11.** Hobah..............	The Church of our fathers.	252	87, 87, 6666, 7. "Ein' feste Burg"	Rejoice to-day with one accord.
249	**11 12, 12 10.** Trisagion............	Holy, holy, holy !	253	87, 887, 77, 77. St. Paul	Worthy of all adoration.
250	**12 10, 11 10.** Venite Adoremus	O, come, all ye faithful.			

HYMN CHANTS.

No.	Name.	Suitable Words.	No.	Name.	Suitable Words.
	For L. M., C. M., or S. M.		V.	Thyatira	One sweetly solemn thought.
I.	Worcester Chant..	O God of hosts.	VI.	Sardis	I thought upon my sins.
II.	Ephesus	This is the day the Lord.	VII.	(5 lines). Philadelphia	Come, labour on !
III.	Smyrna	O God, our help in ages past.			
IV.	*For other Measures of four lines.*		VIII.	(6 lines). Laodicea............	Long did I toil.
	Pergamos	The strain upraise of joy.			

		Date.
Chant Service for Te Deum	W. H. Havergal	1868.
Six Psalm Chants	W. H. Havergal	1863.
Six Kyries	W. H. Havergal	1863-1868.
Six Glorias	W. H. Havergal	1856-1866.
Ter Sanctus	W. H. Havergal	1836.

xvii

V.

[243]

INDEX OF HYMNS

IN

"Songs of Grace and Glory"

SUITABLE FOR EACH TUNE.

xviii   *Index of Hymns in "Songs of Grace and Glory."* [244]

[245]

Index of Hymns in " Songs of Grace and Glory."   xix

After the "Index of Hymns in *Songs of Grace and Glory* Suitable for Each Tune" in pages i–xx, an advertisement page was given next in the original Cocks edition. This advertisement page is found on page 1025 of Volume V of the Havergal edition.

[247]

TABLE OF CHANTS.

————◆•●•◆————

[NOTE.—The sainted Author of the "*Century of Chants*" arranged them simply in order of keys. That arrangement has not been altered, but the following table will facilitate the selection of suitable Chants for each Canticle or Psalm.—F. R. H.]

I.—JUBILANT......................
- Single—Nos. 8, 12, 16, 17, 18, 22, 23, 41.
- Double—Nos. 61, 71, 75, 78, 88, 96, 98.

II.—CHEERFUL. ....
- Single—Nos. 3, 6, 11, 13, 26, 27, 36, 38, 39, 42, 43.
- Double—Nos. 65, 74, 79, 83, 90, 95, 100.

III.—MODERATE.
- (Sweet)
  - Single—Nos. 2, 4, 5, 10, 19, 20, 21, 30, 31, 33, 34, 37, 40, 49, 52, 58.
  - Double—Nos. 69, 73, 80, 82, 86, 97.
- (Solid)
  - Single—Nos. 1, 9, 24, 32, 35, 46, 47, 50, 51, 53, 54, 56, 57, 59, 60.
  - Double—Nos. 62, 63, 64, 67, 68, 72, 76, 81, 84, 87, 89, 91, 92, 93, 94, 99.

IV.—GRAVE ......
- Major.
  - Single—Nos. 7, 48.
  - Double—Nos. 66, 70.
- Minor.
  - Single—Nos. 3, 13, 14, 15, 16, 25, 26, 27, 28, 29, 34, 44, 45, 55.
  - Double—Nos. 77, 85, 88.

CHANGEABLE CHANTS. 3, 13, 16, 26, 27, 34, 88.

(7) Faithful to His Covenant.

368. Heb. X. 15, 23. The Holy Ghost. — "He is faithful that promised".

Tryphosa. 886.

To Thee, O Comforter Divine,
For all Thy grace and power benign,
    Sing we Alleluia!.

To Thee, whose faithful love had place   both
In God's great covenant of grace,
    Sing we Alleluia

To Thee, whose faithful voice doth win
The wandering from the ways of sin,
    Sing we Alleluia

To Thee whose faithful power doth heal,
Enlighten, sanctify, and seal,
    Sing we Alleluia.

To Thee whose faithful truth is shown
By every promise made our own,
    Sing we Alleluia

To Thee, Our Teacher & our Friend,
Our faithful Leader to the end,
    Sing we Alleluia.

To Thee, by Jesus Christ sent down,
Of all His gifts the sum and crown,
    Sing we Alleluia.

To Thee, who art with God the Son,
And God the Father ever one,
    Sing we Alleluia!

August 11. 3. p.m.   Frances Ridley Havergal. 1872

This is another manuscript apparently written in Frances' work with Rev. Snepp on Grace and Glory by her and Rev. Snepp (part of another one is found on page 376 of Volume V). This is the top of the first page of a three-page manuscript in F.R.H.'s handwriting, with also the bottom of the third page. This was hymn number 368 in Songs of Grace and Glory *(on page 705 of Volume V).*

Note: This was another blank page in the original book.

[249]

A CENTURY OF CHANTS

(Sixty Single and Forty Double)

BY

THE REV. W. H. HAVERGAL, M.A.

HONORARY CANON OF WORCESTER.

In the Robert Cocks 1871 First Edition, at this point there were the next six pages, four pages of "Prefatory Notes" by W.H.H. and the two-page "Supplemental Note" on Dr. Crotch. These six pages are added to the Nisbet edition here, numbered [249a] to [249f].

𝔓𝔯𝔢𝔣𝔞𝔱𝔬𝔯𝔶 𝔑𝔬𝔱𝔢𝔰.   [249 a]

IN the year 1836, the Author of this little work published "A Hundred Double Antiphonal Chants, with Remarks on Chants and Chanting." The Remarks met with approbation, and were often quoted. The Chants were composed on a principle, which, though vaguely entertained, had never been defined. The principle was this:—That as Single Chants are used antiphonally, and are, therefore, regarded as echoes of themselves, so Double Chants, especially when sung in halves by the two sides of a choir, should bear a responsive relation between their former and latter half. The statement of this principle greatly interested Dr. Crotch, and met with general assent.

After the publication of the Chants, they were searchingly examined by Dr. Crotch, who amended some, and commended others. In terms not to be repeated, he specially noticed No. 4, which in the present Century is No. 71.

Thirteen years after, *i.e.*, in 1849, the Composer had so far modified his views as to issue the following Memorandum, to be affixed, as far as practicable, to every extant copy of the work.

"SUBSEQUENT NOTE.

"THE Chants in this volume obtained much favour shortly after their publication, in 1836. But the Author, now in 1849, utterly repudiates the great mass of them. He would gladly consign at least ninety of them to the fire, and willingly halve the remaining ten. In some respects, they were, doubtless, an advance upon the trash which had for some time preceded them; but, compared with better models, which the Author has learned to appreciate, they now appear to him to be too light, 'PRETTY,' and secular, to merit ecclesiastical use.
"WORCESTER, *March 14th*, 1849."

About two years afterwards, or full fifteen years from the original date, a somewhat notable Professor, ignoring the previous Memorandum, not only published a bitter and sarcastic censure on the Chants, but fell into the grievous error of representing them as only just published. The case was referred to a mutual arbiter of high standing; but the Professor, though promptly certified of his error, had not the heart in any degree to amend it.

The Chants now published are selected from a large accumulation occasioned by the habit of mental composition during the broken nights and partially sightless days of many a past year. The Author has had to learn that mental

Prefatory Notes. [249 6] iii

music, like mental arithmetic, is often more irksome than profitable, because not easily banished at pleasure.

This brief "APOLOGIA PRO MEIS CANTIBUS," may fairly disarm younger men from censuring the production of so many Chants by one individual.*

The Chants themselves are certainly, but not ostentatiously, intended to illustrate a sort of *beau-ideal* as to what Chants ought to be. Every sound scholar knows that too many correct Chants contain neither sympathy nor skill. They seem to aim at the sensational or pretty, rather than at what is graceful and good. A far too common practice is the unnecessary introduction of discords, the placing of high melodies or their harmonies on reciting notes, and especially the forcing in of the minor seventh on the penultimate of every cadence. This last offence was studiously avoided by older worthies, not only because of its secularity, but because its constant iteration palls the ear.

It may, therefore, be frankly averred, that the present Chants are sent forth in determined opposition to prevailing modernisms. They are intended to be tuneful, but strictly grammatical; symmetrical, also, but not stiff. Doubtless, other eyes will detect failures which the Composer overlooks. He will most gratefully welcome any kind suggestions.

As it has become extremely difficult, if not impossible, to invent a *new* short phrase in vocal music, the most eligible way of arriving at any sort of originality is by a fresh combination of existing, but not over-familiar phrases. How this has been attempted, will presently appear.

The Double Chants† are constructed on the principle already defined. The Single Chants are framed upon virtually the same model; consequently the latter half of each presents some sort of response to the former half. This is

---

* Mr. John Jones, Organist of St. Paul's Cathedral (*circ.* 1780), composed and published "Sixty Chants Single and Double." They were extensively used, though now seldom heard. A few commendatory touches might restore many of them to a fair position. The Octave Chant, A, F♯, D, A, No. 24, said to be the first of its kind, was long the most popular Chant in the kingdom.

† So rarely were Double Chants heard before the present century, that only four were in use at York Minster. The Old Hundredth Tune, "*Chantified*," was used to four verses consecutively of the longer Psalms. These facts were attested by the late Jonathan Gray, Esq., who devoted much attention to the Clock and Choir of the Minster.

The editor still adheres to his published statement, as to the original *use* of the Double Chant, viz., that it was accidentally introduced by a clever, but "idle apprentice," at Gloucester Cathedral, about the middle of the last century.

generally effected by the Bass of the latter half repeating in canon, more or less free, the melody of the former half, or *vice versa.*

This device is pleasing to intelligent eyes and ears, and accords with the Hebrew method of chanting the Psalms antiphonally; only not verse against verse, as is the modern custom, but the half verse against the former, or fellow part of a verse.

Mention has been made of that excellent man and great musician, the late Dr. Crotch. As no record is known to be extant of his views in later life, respecting either his own Chants, or the construction of Chants generally, it may interest some readers to learn the substance of certain letters from him, not long before his sudden and lamented death.*

The worthy Doctor regretted that several Chants of his, never intended for publication, had been printed in various collections. He believed† that they had been surreptitiously copied from certain scrap-books left in the organ-loft of Christ Church, Oxford, and which *used to be* easily accessible to casual visitors. He was inclined to modify, or even ignore, certain Chants which he had either published himself, or had allowed to be published by other persons. He especially instanced his well-known Recte et Retro Chant in G, and his other equally popular Chant in C, beginning with Soper's phrase C, E, D, C. The former he considered faulty by its commencing on a non-fundamental chord, followed by too much similar progression; then, by reciting on a note too low in the Bass; and further, by passing from the third to the fourth strain, with a bare escape from the charge of consecutive fifths. The other Chant he regarded as too wide in compass, too low in two of its Bass reciting notes, and altogether not sufficiently compact.

The judicious Doctor intensely disliked everything *appoggiatural* in Chants, as characteristically secular and unecclesiastical. He equally disliked what he called *streams of crotchets*, in the melody of a Chant; and deprecated all but the simplest discords; and even of them the fewer the better. But a discord on a reciting note was to him intolerable; and one on a terminal note was not much otherwise. He was of opinion that it is not desirable to frame a perfect cadence in

---

* Most of these letters were irretrievably damaged by deluging rains penetrating an unheeded closet, in a Parsonage house. The substance of them, however, is clearly remembered, and has often been narrated in domestic conversations.

† The Author can corroborate this belief by what he once saw with his own eyes.

Prefatory Notes.

[249d]

the middle of a Double Chant, nor to place in any Chant a reciting note higher than D in the Treble, nor lower than A in the Bass.* Were he now living, his reverence for divine things would, doubtless, prompt him to censure the indecent speed with which chanting is too frequently performed. Well will it be when the choristers of our Cathedrals, and the lads who take part in Choral Unions, are taught to chant the Psalms, not only with facility and precision, but with due reverence and spiritual "understanding." Every sound Churchman must desire their careful and uniform instruction, as to where and how the Psalms refer to Him, who not only knew how to chant them, but who said, "*All things must be fulfilled which are written in the Psalms concerning* ME."

W. H. H.

PYRMONT VILLA, LEAMINGTON,
January, 1870.

* This rule as to D in the Treble may, perhaps, be slightly exceeded on spirited occasions. For physical reasons, a higher pitched Chant is more eligible for the evening than for the morning. Not a few Organists and Choir-Masters seem to be unconscious of this fact.

Note: This "Supplemental Note" was written by W.H.H. This refers to Dr. William Crotch (1775–1847), a rarely gifted man, an alumnus and professor of Oxford University, where W.H.H. graduated with B.A. in 1816 and M.A. in 1818.

[249 e]

Supplemental Note.

DR. CROTCH, born at Norwich in 1775, was, as to musical genius, a child of European celebrity. A synoptical account of his singular precocity, and of his subsequent history up to the date of his Oxford Professorship, at the early age of twenty-two, may be found in the "Dictionary of Musicians." But the remarkable points of his later life do not appear to have met with any record. The knowledge of them is now confined to a very limited circle of surviving friends. The Author of the present work ventures, therefore, on a brief narration of such facts as came within the range of his own observation.

The diminutive frame and noble head of Dr. Crotch were types of his feeble health and masterly talent. His modesty was as great as his talent. He was not a man of enterprise or competition, and, consequently, profited less by his powers than many an inferior contemporary. His writings and compositions were pretty much left to make their own way. Although his published works generally fetch a high second-hand price, yet their real merit is not popularly known. They await a literary resurrection.

The Doctor's manual facilities were unique. He could write with his left hand as easily as with his right; and even with both hands at once, when penning the Treble and Bass of a piece of music. Specimens of this ambidexterity can be shown. Though he could not span more than an octave, and organ Pedals were unknown, yet his extemporaneous Basses were not only flowing, but singularly full and fine. By an almost legerdemain use of his fingers and knuckles, he could—as when a child—produce astonishing effects. From his boyhood, he could manipulate a violin, in almost every imaginable position. He occasionally played a duet with one or other of the great Cramers—father or son—in the Hanover Square Rooms.

He had, also, remarkable tact in sketching views and etching them. He published "Six Views in the Neighbourhood of Oxford," and six others of "The Fire at Christ Church." For a short time, and, as he said, "for *fun*," he taught drawing in a ladies' boarding-school, while some ordinary master taught music. He was well-known as extremely clever in pencilling a person's likeness to the very life, while holding a short conversation with him. The Great

Supplemental Note. [249 f]   vii

Walk in Christ Church Meadows used not unfrequently to witness his skill as a pyrotechnist. Some of his devices were not only very elegant, but very original; not a few of them are unconsciously perpetuated in the firework displays of the present times.

What was far better, no auditor in the University Church was more attentive than he; nor could any one surpass him in giving an account of some memorable sermon. It was no uncommon thing for him, while seated in the organ-loft, to take short-hand notes, and to append to them a vivid profile of the preacher.

Summarily, it may be remarked, that the genuine merits of Dr. Crotch were never, during his life, adequately appreciated. His retiring disposition might, in some degree, account for this. They who knew him intimately will ever remember him affectionately; and they who heard his organ or pianoforte performances will never forget that union of brilliancy and majesty, precision and power, which they uniformly presented. "Strange," said a friend, "that a form so diminutive can produce sounds so mighty." "Never," said another, "did I perceive the beauties of the 'Hailstone Chorus' till I heard him play it, on one of Broadwood's grand pianofortes, at the Surrey Institution. It seemed as though I heard the hailstones *rattle* and saw the fire *run along* the ground. No orchestra ever produced an effect at once so vivid and so thrilling."

Dr. Crotch, as our most learned and most accomplished English musician, merits such a memorial as is not yet extant.

W.H.H.'s daughter Miriam wrote this in her biography: "When an Oxonian [a member of Oxford University] my father had the advantage of hearing Dr. Crotch on the organ in his best days, and of imbibing his musical ideas, for which he always retained the utmost veneration. In later years Dr. Crotch often expressed his high opinion of my father's compositions, and his respect for his judgement and learning." —quoted from *Records of the Life of Rev. William Henry Havergal, M.A.* by Jane Miriam Crane (London: Home Words Publishing Office, 1882), original book page 195, page 632 of Volume IV of the Havergal edition.

See more details on Dr. William Crotch on pages 1485–1486 of Volume V of the Havergal edition, and a portrait of him on the next page (410).

[250]

Dr. William Crotch (1775–1847). After W. H. H.'s "Supplemental Note" on the previous two pages, see also pages 1485–1486 of Volume V.

Note : This was another blank page in the original book.

[251]

SINGLE CHANTS.

SINGLE CHANTS. [252]

No. 1.

No. 2.

No. 3.

Changeable.

No. 4.

SINGLE CHANTS. [253]

No. 5.

No. 6.

No. 7.

No. 8.

SINGLE CHANTS.   [254]

No. 9.

No. 10.

No. 11.

No. 12.

SINGLE CHANTS.

[255]

No. 13.

Changeable.

No. 14.

No. 15.

No. 16.

Changeable.

SINGLE CHANTS.   [256]

No. 17.

No. 18.

No. 19.

No. 20.

SINGLE CHANTS.   [257]

No. 21.

No. 22.

No. 23.

No. 24.

SINGLE·CHANTS.   [258]

No. 25.

No. 26.   *Changeable.*

No. 27.   *Changeable.*

No. 28.

SINGLE CHANTS. [257]

No. 29.

No. 30.

No. 31.

No. 32.

SINGLE CHANTS.   [260]

No. 33.

No. 34.   *Changeable.*

No. 35.

No. 36.

SINGLE CHANTS.

[261]

No. 37.

No. 38.

No. 39.

No. 40.

SINGLE CHANTS.   [262]

No. 41.

No. 42.

No. 43.

No. 44.

SINGLE CHANTS.   [263]

No. 45.

No. 46.

No. 47.

No. 48.

SINGLE CHANTS. [264]

No. 49.

No. 50.

No. 51.

No. 52.

SINGLE CHANTS. [265]

SINGLE CHANTS. [266]

[267]

DOUBLE CHANTS.

DOUBLE CHANTS. [268]

No. 61.

No. 62.

DOUBLE CHANTS. [269]

No. 63.

No. 64.

DOUBLE CHANTS.

[270]

No. 65.

Worcester Festival, 1857.

No. 66.

DOUBLE CHANTS.   [271]

No. 67.

No. 68.

DOUBLE CHANTS.   [272]

No. 69

No. 70.

DOUBLE CHANTS.

No. 71.

Recte et Retro.
Worcester Festival, 1845.
(Opening of the New Cathedral Organ.)

No. 72.

DOUBLE CHANTS.

No. 73.   [274]

No. 74.

DOUBLE CHANTS.

[275]

No. 75.

Worcester Festival, 1854.

No. 76.

DOUBLE CHANTS.   [276]

No. 77.

No. 78.

DOUBLE CHANTS. [277]

No. 79.

No. 80.

DOUBLE CHANTS.   [278]

No. 81.
                                                              RECTE ET RETRO.

No. 82.
                                                              RECTE ET RETRO.

DOUBLE CHANTS.

[279]

No. 83.

No. 84.

DOUBLE CHANTS.   [280]

No. 85.

No. 86.

DOUBLE CHANTS.   [281]

No. 86 (a)

ANOTHER OF THE SAME.
(Less contrapunctal but more consistent.)

No. 87.

Q

DOUBLE CHANTS.   [282]

No. 88.

CHANGEABLE.

No. 89.

DOUBLE CHANTS.

No. 90.

[283]

No. 91.

DOUBLE CHANTS.   [284]

No. 92.

No. 93.

DOUBLE CHANTS.

[285]

No. 94.

No. 95.

DOUBLE CHANTS.

[286]

No. 96.

Worcester Festival, 1848.

No. 97.

DOUBLE CHANTS.

[287]

No. 98.

Worcester Festival, 1851.

No. 99.

DOUBLE CHANTS.   [288]

No. 100.

[289]

MUSICAL APPENDIX

TO

HAVERGAL'S PSALMODY,

[290]

MUSICAL APPENDIX.

PREFATORY NOTE.

THE Musical Appendix contains—

(1.) Tunes composed, by request of the Editor of *Songs of Grace and Glory*, for certain hymns requiring special tunes.

(2.) Tunes, old or recent, most of which are contained in the majority of our leading collections, and have obtained a general footing in the Church. The older ones have been harmonized as nearly as possible in accordance with the principles of *Old Church Psalmody*.

(3.) A few tunes inseparably wedded to hymns much used in Missions and Evangelistic services. As these are *not* intended for ordinary church use, no attempt has been made to alter their popular form and slighter harmonizations.

(4.) A few additional tunes for *Songs of Grace and Glory for the Young*, chiefly for new hymns in the enlarged edition.

The Editor of *Songs of Grace and Glory* gratefully acknowledges the kind permission of composers and owners for the use of copyright tunes, as specified in the Index.

"Serve the Lord with gladness, and come before His presence with singing."

254   **EPENETUS.**   (18 6, 13 6, 13 13, 13 15.)

Tell it out a - mong the hea - then that the Lord is King!

Tell it out! Tell it out! that the Lord is King!

Tell it out! Tell it out! Tell it out!

Tell it out! Tell it out!

See Hymn 165.

[291]

Tell it out a-mong the na-tions, bid them shout and sing!

Tell it out! Tell it out! bid them shout and sing!

out!

Tell it out! Tell it out! Tell it out!

FINE.

Tell it out! Tell . . . . it out!

Tell it out! that He shall in-crease;
Tell it out with a-do-ra-tion that He shall in-crease;

Tell it out! that He shall in-crease;

That the migh-ty King of Glo-ry is the King of Peace;

Tell it out with ju-bi-la-tion though the waves may roar, That He

D.S.

sit-teth on the wa-ter-floods, our King for e-ver-more. Tell it

255   EUODIAS.   (8 4, 8 4, 8 8 8, 4)   [292]

See Hymn 428. Also 101.

256   TERTIUS.   (11 11, 11 11, 5.)

See Hymn 525.

[293]

That Thine is the Power, the Power, the Power, the Power!

That Thine, Thine, Thine is the Power, the Power, the Power!

257   **ONESIMUS.** (7 4, 7 4. D.)

See Hymn 695.

258   **CHURCH TRIUMPHANT.**   **(L.M.)**   [294]

See Hymn 1023.   Also 152, 412.

259   **St. GREGORY.**   **(L.M.)**

See Hymn 178.

260   **HURSLEY.**   **(L.M.)**

See Hymn 901.

261   MILES' LANE. (C.M.)   [295]

See Hymn 324.

262   WINTON. (C.M.) (Winchester in the Alto.)

See Hymn 730.

263   St. PETER. (C.M.)

See Hymn 162.

264   St. FLAVIAN. (C.M.)   [296]

See Hymn 145.

265   St. GEORGE. (S.M.)

See Hymn 456.

266   JULIUS. (447,887.)

See Hymn 89.

267   RABENLEI.   (65, 65.)   [297]

See Hymn 1115.   Also 1120.

268   BOHEMIA.   (65, 65, D.)

See Hymn 964.   Also 569.

269   **GROSVENOR.** (65, 65, D.)   [298]

See Hymn 934.

270   **EDGBASTON.** (65, 65, D.)

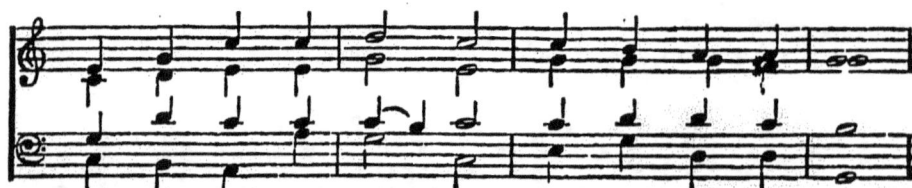

See Hymn 955.

[299]

271 NATIONAL ANTHEM. (664,6664.)

See Hymn 845.

272   St. JOHN. (66, 66, 88.)   [300]

See Hymn 276.

273   BEVAN. (6666, 88.)

See Hymn 275. Also 692.

[301]

274   DARWELL.   (6 6, 6 6, 88.)

See Hymn 827.

275   St. ALPHEGE.   (7 6, 7 6.)

See Hymn 958.

276   CRÜGER.   (76, 76, D.)   [302]

See Hymn 330.

277   St. THEODULPH.   (76, 76, D.)

(1st and 2nd strains may be repeated, and last two omitted or used as Chorus.)

See Hymn 929.

[303]

Ho - san -na, loud Ho - san - na! Ho - san - na, Lord, we sing.

278   **BOSTON.**   (7 6, 7 6. D.)

See Hymn 1138.

279   MUNICH. (76, 76. D.)   [304]

See Hymn 5. Also 8.

280   GOLDSTERN. (76, 76. D.)

See Hymn 1001. Part i.

[305]

281   OLYMPAS.   (7 6, 7 6, 7 7, 7 6.)

See Hymn 635.

282   PHEBE. (77, 66.)   [306]

See Hymn 1068.

283   FILITZ. (777, 5.)

See Hymn 132. Also 900.

284   HARTS. (77, 77.)

See Hymn 629.

285 PLEYEL. (77,77.) [307]

See Hymn 829.

286 HEATHLANDS. (77,77,77.)

See Hymn 410. Also 1028.

287   **DIX.**   (77,77,77.)   [308]

See Hymn 207.

288   **REDHEAD.**   (77,77,77,77.)

See Hymn 462.

289   **St. GEORGE.**   (ELVEY.)   (77,77. D.)

See Hymn 850.

[309]

290   St. HILDA.   (7 7 7 7, D.)

See Hymn 440.

291   HONIDON. (7 7 7 7, D.)   [310]

See Hymn 702. Also 577.

292   URBANE. (8 5, 8 3.) (See No. 262.)

See Hymn 1057.

PART II; or CHORUS. [311]

See Hymn 1048 for Part ii. only.

293 LUCIUS. (86, 889.)

See Hymn 1041.

CHORUS (optional).

294   CANTERBURY. (87, 87.)   [3/2]

See Hymn 1040.

295   SHARON. (87, 87.)

See Hymn 721.

296   GOTHA. (87, 87.)

See Hymn 784.

297   **CORFE MULLEN.** (87, 87, 47.)   [3/3]

See Hymn 135. Also 612.

298   **ALL SAINTS.** (87, 87, 77.)

See Hymn 288. Also 694.

299   **REGENT SQUARE.**   (87 87, 87.)   [3/4]

See Hymn 827.

300   **MAGDEBURG.**   (87, 87, 87; or, 87, 87, 77.)

See Hymn 304.   Also 1086.

301 CIVITAS REGIS MAGNI. (87, 87, 87.) [3/5]

See Hymn 405. Also 671.

302 ORIEL. (87, 87, 87.)

See Hymn 605.

303 MANNHEIM. (87, 87, 87.)

See Hymn 407.

304   St. WERBERGH. (87, 87, 87.)   [3/6]

See Hymn 301

305   DISMISSAL. (87, 87, 87.)

See Hymn 817.

[3/7]

306 FREYLINGHAUSEN. (87, 87. D.)

See Hymn 403. Also 406.

304 St. WERBERGH. (87, 87, 87.) [318]

See Hymn 801

305 DISMISSAL. (87, 87, 87.)

See Hymn 817.

[3/9]

306   **FREYLINGHAUSEN.** (87, 87. D.)

See Hymn 403.   Also 406.

307   St. ASAPH. (87, 87. D.)   [320]

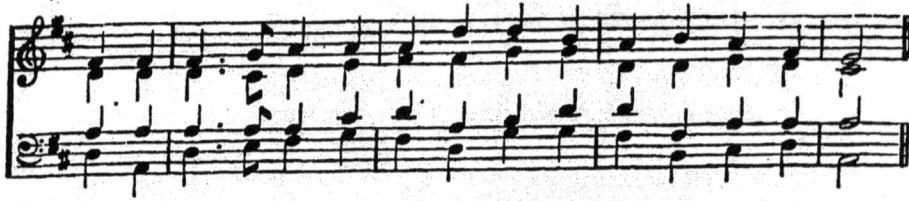

See Hymn 264.

308   EVERTON. (87, 87. D.)

See Hymn 7

[32]

309   **HOLY VOICES.**   (87, 87. D.)

See Hymn 438.

310   BRIDEHEAD. (886.)   [322]

See Hymn 183.

311   HYMN CHANT.

See Hymn 891.

312   ZION. (88, 88, 88.)

See Hymn 429.   Also 616, 617, 702,

[323]

313 EATON. (88, 88, 88.)

See Hymn 181.

314   HALLE. (8 8, 8 8, 8 8.)   [324]

See Hymn 377.

315   DEPTFORD. (10 10, 10 10.)

See Hymn 673.   Also 446.

[325]

316   PYRMONT.   (10, 10, 10, 10.)

See Hymn 696.   Also 666.

317   IRISH.   (11 8, 11 8.)

For Hymn 531 slur 1st and 2nd bars.

See Hymn 458.

[326]

318 **EPAPHRODITUS.** (18 11, 18 12.)

See Hymn 982.

319 **GAIUS.** (11, 10, 11, 10.)

See Hymn 614.

For Evangelistic Services.

[327]

320 "SAFE IN THE ARMS OF JESUS." (76,76,76,76.)

See Hymn 1070.

---

321 "KNOCKING." (77,87,87.)

See Hymn 1053.

[328]

322 "JESUS OF NAZARETH PASSETH." (88,88,89.)

See Hymn 1039.

---

323 "HOLD THE FORT." (85, 85, 85, 85.)

418

[329]

CHORUS.

See Hymn 1062.

324 "THE GREAT PHYSICIAN." (87, 87, 77, 76.)

CHORUS.

See Hymn 1059.

E E 2

419

[330]

325 "ONE MORE DAY'S WORK." (76, 55, 646, 77, 76.)

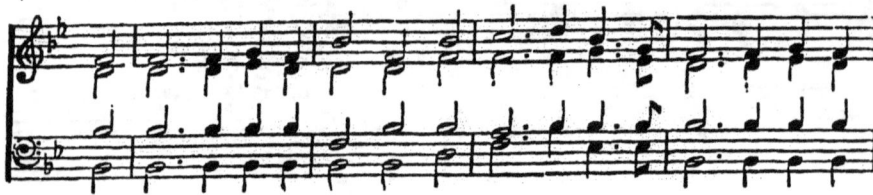

CHORUS.

See **Hymn 1069.**

326 "MORE TO FOLLOW." (76, 76, 76, 76, 66, 76.)

420

[331]

CHORUS.

See Hymn 1061.

327 **"'TIS BETTER FARTHER ON."** (9 7, 8 7, 8 7, 8 7, 10 10.)

CHORUS.

See Hymn 1056.

For Children's Hymns.

[332]

328   JUNIA. (5 6, 5 6.)

See Hymn 131 in "Songs of Grace and Glory" for the Young.

329   KOCKER. (7 6, 7 6.)

See Hymn 55 in "Songs of Grace and Glory" for the Young.

330   DURHAM. (7 7, 7 7.)

See Hymn 138 in "Songs of Grace and Glory" for the Young.

331   **FORTUNATUS.** (8 8 8 8, 6 8, 8 8, 6 8.)   [333]

See Hymn 116 in " Songs of Grace and Glory " for the Young.

332·   **APPHIA.** (9 8, 9 8.)

VERSE 1 AND CHORUS.   FINE.

VERSE 2, &c.   D.C. CHORUS.

See Hymn 87 in " Songs of Grace and Glory " for the Young.

423

333   EUNICE. (10 10, 10 10.)   [334]

See Hymn 54 in "Songs of Grace and Glory" for the Young.

334   "BRIGHT JEWELS." (11 11, 11 11.)

CHORUS.

See Hymn 97 in "Songs of Grace and Glory" for the Young.

424

INDEX OF TUNES IN APPENDIX. [335]

No.	Tune.	No. of Hymns.	No.	Tune.	No. of Hymns.
298	All Saints	288, 694.	328	Junia	131 "S.G.G. for Young."
332	Apphia	87 "S.G.G. for Young."			
			329	Kocker	55 "S.G.G. for Young."
273	Bevan	275, 692.	321	"Knocking"	1053.
268	Bohemia	569, 964.			
278	Boston	1038.	293	Lucius	1041.
310	Bridehead	183.			
334	"Bright Jewels"	97 "S.G.G. for Young."	300	Magdeburg	304, 463, 1086.
			303	Mannheim	407.
294	Canterbury	1040.	261	Miles Lane	324.
258	Church Triumphant	152, 412, 1023.	326	"More to Follow"	1061.
301	Civitas Regis	405, 671.	279	Munich	5, 8.
297	Corfe Mullen	135, 612.			
276	Crüger	330.	271	National Anthem	845.
274	Darwell	827.	281	Olympas	635.
315	Deptford	573.	325	"One more day's"	1069.
305	Dismissal	817.	257	Onesimus	695.
287	Dix	207.	302	Oriel	605.
330	Durham	138 "S.G.G. for Young."			
			282	Phebe	1068.
313	Eaton	181.	285	Pleyel	829.
270	Edgbaston	955.	316	Pyrmont	696, 666.
318	Epaphroditus	982.			
254	Epenetus	165.	267	Rabenlei	1115, 1120.
333	Eunice	54 "S.G.G. for Young."	288	Redhead	462.
255	Euodias	101, 428.	299	Regent Square	327.
308	Everton	7.			
			320	"Safe in the arms"	1070.
283	Filitz	132, 900.	295	Sharon	721.
331	Fortunatus	116 "S.G.G. for Young."	275	St. Alphege	958.
306	Freylinghausen	403, 406.	307	St. Asaph	264.
			264	St. Flavian	145.
319	Gaius	614.	289	St. George (Elvey)	850.
280	Goldstern	1001 (Part I.).	265	St. George	456.
296	Gotha	784.	259	St. Gregory	178.
324	"Great Physician"	1059.	290	St. Hilda	440.
269	Grosvenor	934.	272	St. John	276, 1030.
			263	St. Peter	162.
314	Halle	377.	277	St. Theodulph	929.
284	Harts	629.	304	St. Werbergh	301.
286	Heathlands	410, 1028.			
323	"Hold the Fort"	1062.	256	Tertius	525.
309	Holy Voices	438.	327	"'Tis better farther on"	1056.
291	Honidon	577, 702.	311	Troyte's Hymn Chant	891.
260	Hursley	901.			
			292	Urbane II.	1048, 1057.
317	Irish	458, 531.			
			262	Winton	730.
322	"Jesus of Nazareth"	1039.			
266	Julius	89.	312	Zion	429, 616, 617, 792.

Preface to *Songs of Grace and Glory* by Charles Busbridge Snepp and Frances Ridley Havergal

Extremely few people today realize the remarkably fine gifts Frances Ridley Havergal had in music. As a performer and as a composer she had a rare level of gifts, and she had rare diligence with her gifts. Her father, Rev. William Henry Havergal, was the foremost church musician and composer of sacred music in England in his generation, and he was a leading advocate for reform in the practice and taste of church music. Rev. Charles Busbridge Snepp, an Anglican pastor, was a hymnologist with a very important collection of hymnbooks, a deep interest in hymns, and a desire to bring out a new, comprehensive hymnal. Snepp had written to William Henry about this project, and on the morning of W.H.H.'s last conscious day, he composed a tune for a hymn in Snepp's new project, *Songs of Grace and Glory*. The next day, April 17, 1870, Easter, he was seized with apoplexy and never regained consciousness, dying on April 19. Rev. Snepp after that wrote to his daughter, F.R.H., and later they concluded that she would edit the music for the new hymnal.

Though extremely obscure today, *Songs of Grace and Glory* is a true treasure of worship in song, a gold mine strongly worthy to be republished today, studied by church musicians, and used in worship in our day. Snepp was the architect and leader of the work and the editor of the texts, and F.R.H. prepared and edited all the music. She also wrote words and music to several hymns for this hymnal. This is an enormous and enormously impressive body of work. Frances directly prepared for press the scores of 1,100 hymns, and after she thought that her work was completed on this, she learned that the papers and plates for the Appendix at the printer had been lost in a devastating fire, so that she would need to do all the work on the Appendix again. (See the first part of Chapter 11 of *Memorials of Frances Ridley Havergal*, pages 51–52 of this Volume IV of the Havergal edition.) In the British Library, a copy of *Songs of Grace and Glory* is dated 1883 with "Three Hundred and Thirteenth Thousand" on the title page.

The work began with *Havergal's Psalmody and Century of Chants*, a republication of two of William Henry's earlier volumes of hymntunes composed by him, *Old Church Psalmody* (1847) and *A Hundred Psalm and Hymn Tunes* (1859), with other previously unpublished materials by W.H.H. and also a few tunes composed by Frances, all edited by F.R.H. and published by Robert Cocks & Co., London, 1871. Cocks published a second and a third edition (the third edition in 1872). James Nisbet & Co. published the fourth edition in 1877, and this is the definitive edition. *Havergal's Psalmody and Century of Chants* was a "Companion Volume to Songs of Grace and Glory." The music in *H.P.C.C.* was the music for the hymns in *Songs of Grace and Glory*. *Songs of Grace and Glory* was published in a number of editions. The first publication, by William Hunt & Co., London, 1872, had 1025 hymns, and was brought out in eight different formats (varying sizes, leather or cloth covers, 6 indices or 3 indices, with varying prices for each format). Near the back of the hymnal was "Index V. Tunes with Appropriate Hymns." This first publication of *Songs of Grace and Glory* had only the words, without the music, and with this index an organist or pianist could find and play the tune for each hymn in *Songs of Grace and Glory* from the "Accompanying Volume" *Havergal's Psalmody and Century of Chants*. Later James Nisbet & Co. published *S.G.G.*, and in 1876 Nisbet published the "Musical Edition" of *Songs of Grace and Glory*. In 1880 Nisbet published a "New and Enlarged Musical Edition" of the hymnbook, a final re-evaluation and preparation of this by F.R.H. Rev. Snepp wrote in his Preface to this 1880 edition: "The musical Editor, the late beloved Frances Ridley Havergal, after composing several New and Beautiful Tunes, and carefully re-arranging the whole, has been called to join the heavenly choir above. Not, however, until she had first bequeathed to the Church of Christ these results of her matured judgment." F.R.H.'s work on *Songs of Grace and Glory* is very valuable, and her collaboration and friendship with Rev. Snepp were very important in her life. Snepp was both her senior colleague and also her dear friend and brother, and they valuably benefitted and enriched each other, both in the work on the hymnbook and in other ways. The definitively finalized edition of *Songs of Grace and Glory* was published approximately six months after F.R.H. died (June 3, 1879) and six months before Rev. Snepp died (June 23, 1880). David Chalkley, October 20, 2004.

Volume V of *The Complete Works of Frances Ridley Havergal* (entitled *Songs of Truth and Love: Music by Frances Ridley Havergal and William Henry Havergal*) has an extensive set of music composed by William Henry Havergal. Besides the complete *Havergal's Psalmody and Century of Chants*, there are several other scores (published and unpublished) by W.H.H. Given next is a list of those scores by him in Volume V of the Havergal edition. This set is not nearly all of the music that he composed. Almost certainly there were <u>many</u> manuscript scores by him that were never published; how many of these are extant now is not known. There are also published scores by W.H.H. not in this group, which are kept in the British Library in London, and likely a few other British libraries. Also, the Worcester Cathedral Library likely has at least a few of his compositions in manuscript score. The research and wrok on the Havergal edition has been long, costing so much money, time, and effort, exhausting me and depleting me financially and otherwise. I do not mean to complain a trace: to have been given this work was a true privilege and honor from the Lord. Not at all to complain, this was said to explain why more of W.H.H.'s scores were not pursued: because of lack of time, energy, means. His prose works, poetry, and music are a true goldmine, abundantly worthy of research and re-publication, and of doctoral dissertations probing them. A very finely gifted composer (obscure, yet very fine) once said to me about William Henry Havergal's scores, "He is better than me."

List of Music Scores by William Henry Havergal in Volume V of the Havergal Edition

"Just as I am, without one plea" Op. 48 (words by Charlotte Elliott)

"O Thou Dread Power" Op. 42 (words by Burns)

"Poland" Op. 50 (words by William Henry Havergal)

"Gentle Dew" (words by W.H.H.)

"Lord, Build Thy House Speedily" Op. 5 (apparently an English translation of a Hebrew hymn, Adir Hu Yivne veito b'karov, with a Hebrew melody notated and arranged by W.H.H.)

Three Hymns by Reginald Heber Op.10

"From Greenland's Icy Mountains " (words by Reginald Heber) the Robert Cocks score for solo voice and piano published by Robert Cocks & Co.

"From Greenland's Icy Mountains" (words by Reginald Heber) the score for voices with organ or piano published by Novello

Original Airs and Harmonized Tunes Adapted to Hymns of Various Measures, Op. 2 (This was a collection of thirty brief, one-page scores.)

An Evening Service, and a Hundred Antiphonal Chants, Op. 35 (the Novello edition)

An Evening Service, Op. 37

"Acquaint thee with God" Op. 38 (a paraphrase of Job 22:21)

Te Deum and Jubilate, with Chants, Op. 39

An Anthem, "Give Thanks" Op. 40 (I Chronicles 16:8–10)

Excerpts from *Lyra Ecclesiastica* (This was a collection of scores by several composers; the Preface was written by W.H.H, and several of his scores were included in this volume.

The Grand Chant in Forty Different Forms, Op. 52

The Chant and the Psalm Tune, for September 6, 1848

The Chants and the Psalm Tune, for August 26, 1851

Two Chants, for September 5, 1854

Four Double Chants (No. 1 Recte et Retro, No. 2 Double Counterpoint, No. 3 Recte et
  Retro, No. 4 Double Counterpoint and Retrogradation)

Veni Creator

No. 209 "Venite Adoremus"

No. 210 "Winterdyne"

No. 211 "Zared"

No. 212 "Zeboim"

"Non Nobis, Domine" (the first part of Psalm 115:1)

"God Save the Queen" (In Memoriam December 14, 1861) for four voices (words by W.H.H.)

"God Save the Queen" for solo, duet, and trio

"A New National Hymn" for March 10, 1863 (words by W.H.H.)

"Fireside Music" by the Rev. W. H. Havergal, M.A.

"A Christmas Carol" (words by W.H.H.)

"The Bethlehem Shepherd-Boy's Tale" (words by W.H.H.)

"Christmas Carol" (words by W.H.H.)

"Mementote Vinctorum" ("A Musical Inverse Palindrome, Composed for Three Voices")

Enigma No. 23 (words by W.H.H.)

Manuscript "A Gloucester Cry" (Double Antiphonal Chant from a subject "Hot cross buns")

Manuscript "Child's Morning Hymn" August 5, 1843 (words likely by W.H.H.)

Manuscript "Saviour, when from realms above" ("Each Part in Each Strain Per Recte et Retro") Bonn January 18,
  1866 (words by W.H.H.)

Manuscript "Tunes for grandchildren"

Manuscripts "Hark my mother's voice I hear" and "Sleep baby sleep Our cottage vale is deep" for
  his granddaughter, Frances Anna Shaw (words likely by W.H.H.)

Manuscript "Mighty Father ! Blessed Son !" (words by Dr. John S. B. Monsell)

Manuscript "An Identical Inverse Palindrome (to a Missionary Hymnette)"

A Reprint of *All the Tunes in Ravenscroft's Book of Psalms* with Introductory

Remarks by W.H.H. (London: Novello, 1845)

A History of the Old Hundredth Psalm Tune, with Specimens by W.H.H. (New York: Mason Brothers, 1854)

Christmas Carols and Sacred Songs (words only) (London: James Nisbet & Co., 1869)

Words of missionary hymns by W.H.H., sung at meetings on behalf of the Church Missionary Society

"Nuptial Grace" words by W.H.H., to be sung to his score "Eden"

the score entitled "from 'Glory to Glory.' " words by F.R.H. set to music by W.H.H.

FORMS AND PRICES
OF
HAVERGAL'S PSALMODY & CHANTS.
Companion Volume to Songs of Grace & Glory.

		s.	D.
A.	HAVERGAL'S PSALMODY AND CENTURY OF CHANTS, bound in cloth, gilt lettered, with full Prefaces, Indices, and Photographic Portrait	5	0
B.	Ditto, ditto, without Chants	3	6
C.	Chants and Preface alone	1	6

CHEAPER EDITIONS.

		s.	D.
D.	HAVERGAL'S PSALMODY AND CHANTS, without Prefaces and Portrait	1	6
E.	Ditto, Ditto, without Chants	1	0
F.	CHANTS alone, without Preface	0	9

London:
ROBERT COCKS & CO., NEW BURLINGTON STREET, W.
By Special Appointment
Music Publishers to Her Majesty the Queen, H.R.H. the Prince of Wales, and H.I.M. Napoleon III.,
AND THROUGH ALL MUSICSELLERS.

FORMS AND PRICES
OF
SONGS OF GRACE AND GLORY.

		s.	D.
A.	Extra large paper, very superior binding	10	0
B.	Large type, leather gilt	5	0
C.	Large type, cloth gilt and lettered	4	0
D.	Large type, cloth limp	3	6
E.	Small type, leather gilt	2	6
F.	Small type, cloth gilt and lettered	1	6
G.	Small type, cloth limp	1	0

For reduced terms on Editions A. to E., apply to Rev. C. B. Snepp, LL.M., Vicar of Perry Barr, near Birmingham.

"SONGS OF GRACE AND GLORY." A Hymnal, containing 1,025 Hymns for Private, Family, and Public Worship, Edited by the Rev. C. B. SNEPP, LLM., Vicar of Perry Barr. With copious Indices of Authors and Dates, Subjects, Texts, and Tunes; also a Table of Hymns for the Sundays and Holy Days of the Ecclesiastical Year.

London:
WILLIAM HUNT & CO., HOLLES ST., CAVENDISH SQUARE.

This is an advertisement page (after page xx) in the original Robert Cocks edition of Havergal's Psalmody and Century of Chants. Cocks' publication of H.P.C.C. had the music for the hymns in S.G.G., and William Hunt's publication of Songs of Grace and Glory had the words only, without music. Later the words and music were printed together in a "Musical Edition" of S.G.G. This 1880 Nisbet edition of Songs of Grace and Glory is the definitive version, published approximately six months after F.R.H. died (June 3, 1879) and approximately six months before Charles Busbridge Snepp died (June 23, 1880).